Group Therapy Approaches for Working with Criminal Justice Clients

American University & Colleges Press™
American Book Publishing
5442 So. 900 East, #146
Salt Lake City, UT 84117-7204
http://www.american-book.com
Salt Lake City, Utah,
Printed in the United States of America on acid-free paper.

Group Therapy Approaches for Working with Criminal Justice Clients
Designed by Jana Rade, design@american-book.com

Publisher's Note: This publication is designed to provide accurate and authoritative information in regard to the subject matter covered. It is sold or distributed with the understanding that the publisher and author is not engaged in rendering legal, accounting, or other professional service. If legal advice or other expert assistance is required, the services of a competent professional person in a consultation capacity should be sought.

ISBN-13: 978-1-58982-639-7
ISBN-10: 1-58982-639-6

Library of Congress Cataloging-in-Publication Data

Deisler, Francis J.
Group therapy approaches for working with criminal justice clients / Francis J. Deisler.
p. ; cm.
Includes bibliographical references.
ISBN-13: 978-1-58982-639-7 (alk. paper)
ISBN-10: 1-58982-639-6 (alk. paper)
1. Prisoners--Mental health services. 2. Group psychotherapy. I. Title.
[DNLM: 1. Psychotherapy, Group--methods. 2. Criminals--psychology. WM 430 D325g 2010]
RC451.4.P68D45 2010
616.89'1520086927--dc22
2010018688

Group Therapy Approaches for Working with Criminal Justice Clients

Francis J. Deisler, Ph.D.

Preface

I am a private practice clinical psychologist and a clinical social worker who specializes in the assessment and treatment of criminal justice clients. I am also on the teaching staff of the Forensic Training Institute that offers training on the assessment and treatment of general offenders, sex offenders, and domestic violence batterers, as well as offense specific group therapy training. The training goal is to familiarize students and trainees with the treatment needs of criminal offenders. The treatment needs include basic alcohol and drug pharmacology, psychodynamics of sexual offending and domestic violence, assessments, models of offender treatment, and family issues.

In teaching courses and training mental health professionals my colleagues and I were unable to identify any text book that was treatment specific. Most of the writings addressed the diagnosis of the antisocial personality disorder, assessment, and institutional programs. Nothing addressed group therapy approaches or techniques. The purpose of this book is to provide those counselors working with criminal justice clients with the knowledge and information they will need to develop and run an effective group consisting of all criminal justice clients.

When I decided to write this book, I kept in mind the complaints of our trainees and students about the lack of availability of books and literature on specific offender group therapy. To illustrate the application of concepts, I have included some examples from my own clinical practice and experiences.

As with any effort such as this, there were many people involved who offered their expertise and advice resulting in this final product. I want to thank Karla Taylor, M.S, for her assistance in editing, Claudia Timmons for her contribution to the chapter on women's needs, Dr. Kevin Stewart who reviewed the manuscript and made suggestions, and Dr. Bret White for his consultations of sex offender assessment and treatment, and finally, the National Association of Forensic Counselors for their support and endorsement of the book.

Finally, I want to express my appreciation and devotion to my sons, Christopher and Jonathan for reviewing material in their respective areas of expertise.

Table of Contents

Chapter 1: Criteria for the Placement of Criminal Justice Clients in Group Therapy Treatment.................1
Chapter 2: Client Screening and Group Assignment 29
Chapter 3: Group Development 45
Chapter 4: Best Practice Therapies 79
Chapter 5: Stages of Individual Change........................... 113
Chapter 6: Group Treatment Issues & Strategies 129
Chapter 7: Gender Specific Treatment Needs 163
Chapter 8: Dealing with Difficult Grouup Members 183
Chapter 9: After Care and Relapse Prevention................207
References 218

Chapter 1: Criteria for the Placement of Criminal Justice Clients in Group Therapy Treatment

Brief Overview of the Criminal Justice Client

The overwhelming majority of criminal justice clients present with an antisocial personality disorder (APD), substance abuse disorder, or sexual disorder that co-occurs with other co-morbid psychiatric disorders. They rarely seek out treatment for themselves and are usually not very motivated to change. For that reason, motivating a criminal justice client to change their behavior takes a skilled therapist with specialized skills. In therapeutic settings, where criminal justice clients are seen, the therapist who is skillful at motivating their client's change is more effective than one who is skillful working with motivated clients. Unfortunately, for the forensic therapist who works with criminal justice clients, the majority of therapeutic interventions have been developed for use with other disorders and do not work well in most cases. In fact, the majority of mental health professionals don't think a primary diagnosis of APD can be treated at all. However, as difficult as it is to treat APDs, they are not untreatable. There are individuals diagnosed with APD who have, because of their early life experiences, developed differently than most people and have different needs, and as a result they require different intervention techniques in order to change. (Brown, M, 1973) states that "different interventions are needed because their needs are different. The forensic therapist that understands their criminal justice client's needs will be more effective as a change agent than one who does not."

The APDs' pathology appears to be ingrained into their personality as a result of their early developmental problems. No organic pathology is identified, but there is an obvious lack of guilt, anxiety, or other feelings that reflect recognition or responsiveness to internalized social standards. Their acting out behavior is the most common symptom identified, which is used primarily as defense structures to avoid their repressed feelings. These behaviors become deep rooted within the personality and they experience them as being ego-syntonic. For example, they think "That's who I am," or "That's just the way I am." The blocking out of their feelings is so complete that the energy that would ordinarily be used to feel and express their emotions is converted into antisocial acting out behaviors.

The APD, as well as most offenders, do not think they need the type of help the court is offering them because they are not aware of the significance of their unmet needs. They generally consider their unhappiness, negative life experiences, and insensitivity as being part of everyday life that is experienced by everyone. The APD thinks, therefore, that there's nothing to change.

Social Attitudes Towards Ex-Offenders

For the most part, the general public supports the idea that once an individual has paid their debt to society for the crime they committed that it should no longer be held against them if they are truly rehabilitated. Most people agree that the past cannot be changed. The important thing is what the person does with their life in the present.

In 1999, the National Association of Forensic Counselors distributed 6,500 survey questionnaires nationwide in an attempt to establish society's attitude toward ex-offenders and the concept of rehabilitation. Of the 6,500 survey questionnaires distributed, 4,485 or 69% were returned. Of the returned questionnaires, 93% or 4,171 respondents agreed that rehabilitated ex-offenders living pro-social lifestyles should not be discriminated against. The exception was for sexual offenses committed against children. 314 respondents, or 7%, thought that offenders should be discriminated against regardless of the offense or duration of recovery. These results were encouraging. A follow-up survey study of 2,500 criminal court judges was done in February, 2000 in order to determine the attitude of the criminal justice system towards offender rehabilitation and discrimination. Surprisingly, there was a close correlation between the results of both survey studies. Of the 2,500 survey questionnaires distributed across all fifty states, 2,400 or 96% were returned. 2,160 or 90% of the courts surveyed agreed that if rehabilitation was achieved and there were no incidences of re-offending, the rehabilitated offender should not be discriminated against. However, 240 respondents, or 10%, of the sample disagreed (Drury, 2000).

So, what seems to be the problem with ex-offenders re-entering society and seeking a pro-social lifestyle? The primary problem is the federally funded special interest groups that represent themselves as being human service organizations. Those groups create barriers in order to protect their own interests. They lobby and block any legislation that would restore an ex-offender's right to seek licensure in certain professions, even if the ex-offender has been living a pro-social lifestyle for 25 years or more. And yet, they participate on various state governors' task forces on crime and dictate what the criteria should be for programs, treatment, and rehabilitation. The majority of these groups pressure legislatures to pass bills by convincing them that this is what their constituency wants and it is in the best interest of public safety. In reality, many of these special interest groups' bills are only in their own best interest in order to seek further funding and contribute to the recidivism problem which is not in the best interest of public safety. To even further blemish the democratic process, many of the legislatures that become involved in these groups' pursuit of legislation are either members or participants in the special interest groups' activities. This type of behavior on the part of such legislatures should be labeled as malfeasance of office and not in the best interest of public safety.

Many ex-offenders are indeed dangerous because of their personality disorder and do need to be managed, especially those offenders with psychopathic characteristics. However, I also believe that there would be fewer offenders who are not psychopathic re-offending if there were not as many barriers to their full recovery and living a pro-social lifestyle.

Mental health professionals who believe that people can change should become more active and outspoken in order to assure that the offenders that are treated will have the opportunity to carry what they have learned and achieved in treatment into their daily lives. It is also important to prepare the criminal justice client to face the barriers that will be placed before them in their recovery so that they are able to avoid relapse. It is also crucial that they know that the therapist will be available during their crises.

Group Therapy Considered Best Practice

Group therapy for criminal justice clients is intended to assist the offender in identifying the risk factors in their daily lives that contribute to their criminal acting out behavior and to develop alternative strategies of coping to prevent relapsing. Group therapy focuses on the offender's interpersonal difficulties, lack of social skills, cognitive restructuring of their distorted thinking, beliefs and affective style, identifying high-risk factors, solving emotional difficulties and relapse planning. The group therapy approach to treating criminal justice clients provides many therapeutic benefits that could not be accomplished in individual therapy. However, in order for group therapy to be successful with this specific population specialized skills in group screening, referral, group development and technique are required.

Group Therapy vs. Individual Therapy

Group therapy is a powerful therapeutic tool that has pros and cons. The disadvantages of group therapy over individual therapy include:

1. Less time for each group member as opposed to individual therapy.

2. Less confidentiality than individual therapy because of the group setting.
3. Criminal justice clients may know each other from the streets.

However, these are minor disadvantages when compared to the advantages of group therapy. The advantages to group therapy include:

1. Criminal justice clients learn needed social skills faster by observing and reflecting on their own and other group members' social skills.
2. Criminal justice clients present with severe interpersonal relationship problems which can be more effectively addressed in a group setting.
3. Criminal justice clients share similar life problems, risk factors, and are able to express empathy towards each other.
4. Clients receive feedback from their peers about issues and lifestyle problems.
5. Group therapy offers an opportunity to benefit through participation and observation.
6. Group therapy allows the exploration of issues and dynamics in a social context that more accurately reflects the criminal justice clients' real life.
7. Criminal justice clients find it more difficult to con, lie, cheat and manipulate in a group of their peers.
8. Clients have an opportunity to change their lifestyle behaviors through the group process.
9. Clients have an opportunity to learn from each other's mistakes and successes.
10. Emotional and social support may be available

while working through issues in a supportive and confidential environment.

11. Group therapy is less expensive for criminal justice clients who, if employed, usually make a minimal wage.

As you can see, the advantages of group therapy can far outweigh the disadvantages. Group therapy can even outweigh the advantages of individual therapy for the criminal justice client. However, this does not necessarily mean that the client should not be seen on an individual basis. The criminal justice client should be allowed individual sessions if there are truly issues that cannot be shared within the group such as:

1. Issues regarding their sexuality or sexual identity
2. If the client is a witness in another criminal case
3. The client is being pressured by gang members
4. The client is fearful about sharing his past crimes or secret life with a group

Prior to seeing the client individually you will need to carefully assess the legitimacy of the client's request. If their request is granted, depending upon the severity of the issue, the client must agree that at some point, when they do become comfortable with the issue, that they will eventually share it with other group members.

Assessing the legitimacy of requests for individual therapy is important because many criminal justice clients will request individual attention to get over, under and around working on their issues and to make fools of the therapist.

Current Trends in Offender Group Therapy

Most therapists who counsel criminal justice clients, whether in private practice or criminal justice settings, are not highly trained or skillful in group therapy techniques for criminal justice offenders. In fact, very few have undergone any extensive training in group therapy, or for that matter, been supervised by someone with extensive training. They are, for the most part, simply individuals who graduated from a university, became licensed in their profession, secured employment and are expected to do a job. Any competency developed is because they have sought out their own offender treatment training and readings.

Many criminal offender counseling books have become available over the past few years. Most of these books have emphasized effective counselor attitudes and the therapeutic relationship. However, no book has focused on the specialized knowledge, skills and training required to effectively develop an offender group and the skills that are required to effectively treat the offender in a group therapy setting.

The purpose of traditional group therapy has always been to facilitate change in the client's interpersonal behavior as well as in their thoughts, feelings and beliefs about others. In other words, group therapy is an interpersonal milieu for the solution of interpersonal difficulties. This, at first glance, appears to be the perfect treatment for criminal justice clients; however, the majority of criminal justice clients who have been in group therapy continue to experience difficulties in their lives and don't seem to benefit from therapy. This is primarily because most activities for criminal justice clients that are labeled as being group psychotherapy are not oriented toward change. In most offender programs activities that are pointed to as being group psychotherapy are actually psychoeducational groups that are oriented toward the offender gaining knowledge about their life problems and satisfying the mandate of the court that the offender attend counseling rather than making sure that the offender changes. These programs are designed more for the court systems' need for a referral dumping ground and maintaining the offender in the community. Traditionally, this approach has been taken because the attitude of the courts and many mental health professionals has been that there is no hope for most offenders. The basics of forming and developing effective offender groups is ignored and in many cases the therapist is not properly trained in holding group therapy with criminal justice clients because of this hopeless attitude.

In an effective offender group the client explores their criminal behaviors and personal issues in a social context, working through their issues in a supportive, confidential environment where they have the opportunity to both participate and observe by giving and receiving feedback. Unfortunately, this rarely occurs in most offender groups because the current trend in most programs has been to place every criminal justice client referred into a group without screening them or preparing them for group participation. It is essential that criminal justice clients be screened as to their eligibility to participate in group therapy and that the program have a selection criteria for admission to a group. The selection criteria for admission to an offender group may be somewhat different than for a non-offender group, but must be developed in order to make certain that the group can fulfill its mission.

Many offender programs and groups have a tendency to

focus only on the offender's criminal behavior. Very few programs address the psychosocial problems, co-occurring disorders or developmental interferences that may have been contributing to the client's antisocial lifestyle. Just focusing on a particular criminal behavior and not addressing the issues that contribute to the criminal behavior is a recipe for relapse.

Offender Group Selection Criteria

There are a number of approaches to developing selection criteria for traditional groups available, however, none really apply to offender groups or are designed to make certain the group can fulfill its mission. As most forensic counselors already know the majority of clients referred by the criminal justice system present with ego syntonic character pathologies which manifests itself through interpersonal difficulties, criminal acting out behaviors and highly extreme resistance to change. Developing selection criteria for this type of population can be both tricky and extremely difficult. It is doubtful that a criminal justice client with such character pathologies would benefit from being in a group with other group members suffering from depression, anxiety or a neurosis, or even be capable of contributing to the group's mission or goal. A major part of appropriate client selection for group therapy is matching the client up with the mission or goals of a new or existing group. In criminal justice groups the mission or the group's goals must be firmly established and are somewhat different than what would be found in most other groups. Examples of a therapy group's mission or goals can include one or all of the following, or whatever goals or mission the therapist establishes:

1. Clients will identify the high-risk situations contributing to their criminal acting out.
2. Clients will identify their distorted thinking and belief patterns and develop new thoughts and beliefs.
3. Clients will identify their emotions and develop appropriate ways to express them.
4. Clients will learn and practice appropriate social skills.
5. Clients will learn empathy skills.
6. Clients will become and remain alcohol and drug free.
7. Clients will develop effective relapse prevention plans.
8. Clients will participate actively in the group.

These are just a few examples of possible group goals or the mission of a criminal offender group. The counselor may add to, use all, or delete from the above examples according to the purpose and mission of their group and what the group wants to accomplish. In my clinical experience, the ideal criminal justice group therapy candidates are those who:

1. Recognize the existence of their criminal behavior as a problem.
2. Recognize the severity of their behavior on self, family and others.
3. Are willing to consider solutions and alternatives to their antisocial lifestyle.
4. Believe they have the ability to follow through with solving their life problems.
5. Are sick and tired of being sick and tired with their losing life style.

6. Are willing to stay alcohol and drug free during treatment.
7. Are at least of average intelligence.
8. Are not presently taking a prescribed medication that would impair their consciousness during treatment.
9. Acknowledge and accept the group's goals and mission.

Criminal justice clients such as these are not as rare as one might think they are. The reason people don't hear much about this type of criminal justice client is because not very many criminal justice programs have group admission criteria and the clients are not screened prior to participating in a group. Screening clients, who have the above characteristics, and admitting them to group increases the probability that the client, and the group as a whole, will benefit and the therapeutic efficacy of the group will be high.

There must also be criteria for clients that are not appropriate for group therapy. In my experience, the clients that are inappropriate for group therapy participation include:

1. Clients that state they do not want to participate. The client has a right to refuse being placed in a group. Admitting a client into group against their will only creates problems for the client, the therapist and the group. This can only impair the therapeutic efficacy of the group.
2. Clients that suffer from an organic disorder.
3. Clients that are unable to abstain from alcohol or drugs and are assessed as being dependent. These clients must first be detoxed prior to program admission.

4. Clients that are psychotic or are on medication that will impair their state of consciousness. Clients that are actively psychotic require a group which is prepared to deal with their symptoms, delusions or paranoia with techniques designed to deal with their special circumstances, as well as a well trained and skilled therapist.
5. Clients with a paranoid personality disorder.
6. Clients that have poor impulse control or social control. These clients need to be thoroughly assessed as to their level of interpersonal functioning. The client's threat level to others needs to be assessed.
7. Clients that are introverted and have difficulty sharing about themselves.
8. Clients that present with a life crisis which may require individual therapy as opposed to group therapy.

Admitting a client into your group who presents with one or more of the above characteristics is a set up for the client, the group as whole and the therapist to fail. Just as the probability of the therapeutic efficacy of a group is high with those clients that meet the criteria for admission to a group, the therapeutic efficacy of a group is low when admitting a client with the above undesirable characteristics.

What are the options for the client who may not be a good candidate for group therapy? There are a number of different types of groups that have traditionally been used in treating criminal justice clients and substance abusers that a client not eligible for admission to a cognitive-behavioral group can participate in until they do become eligible to participate.

Some of those groups include the following:

1. Social skills development groups can be used to assist the client in improving their interpersonal relationships, anger management, conflict resolution, problem solving, relaxation techniques, time structuring, and other skills needed to get along better with others and to manage their urges to commit a crime or use substances.
2. Psychoeducational groups can be used to educate the client about relationships, living a pro-social life, substance abuse and more.
3. Support group participation such as Offenders Anonymous, Narcotics Anonymous or Alcoholics Anonymous.
4. Focus groups where a single subject is the focus of attention such as relationships, human sexuality, health, dating and more.

Seeing the ineligible client in individual therapy is another way to go, however, this approach is much more expensive. However, the client may not be able to afford individual therapy. Any of these approaches are appropriate. However, in my experience it has always been important to discuss with the client that these steps have been taken in their best interest until they become eligible or comfortable participating in a cognitive-behavioral group. During this period, assessment of the client's ability to fully participate in group therapy continues. Assessment should inquire about the client's willingness to participate in group therapy and how close they now match the ideal client criteria. This may present a problem because the client may have moved close to fulfilling the criteria of an ideal client, but isn't completely ready. The therapist must then decide how much deviation from the ideal client they are willing to accept in making the decision to admit the client into the group. Many times some deviation from the ideal client must be made; however, keep in mind that the further away from the ideal client the therapist wanders, the more difficult it will become for the therapist as well as the other group members. The therapist must keep in mind at all times that the success of the group depends mostly on appropriate admission and that matching a client to a group is critical for both the client's and the group's overall success.

Group Format

Group therapy is considered "best practice" for criminal justice clients with antisocial personality disorder (ASPD), sexual offenders and substance abuse problems. The relationship between alcohol and drug abuse, crime and violence has been clearly established. The Center on Addiction and Substance Abuse recently published an extensive study about this relationship. It was determined that 80% of adult inmates were under the influence at the time they committed their crimes, engaged in illegal activity to buy drugs, had a history of drug or alcohol abuse, or some combination of these factors (Fisher and Harrison, 2000). This creates a problem during assessment and the screening interview to figure out which group the client will fit into best.

Criminal justice offender groups are homogeneous in nature because all of the members have committed a criminal offense. However, the groups must be more uniform in composition, if at all possible, in order to function effectively as follows:

1. Males and females are treated in separate groups. Mixing male and female offenders in the same group doesn't work well because the therapist and the agency's liability are high if a romance occurs between a male and female client. Same sex groups are more effective for females because they have different treatment needs than males. Females are more likely to have been sexually abused, emotionally abused, physically abused, have a major affective disorder, anxiety or a post-traumatic stress disorder.
2. Clients diagnosed with antisocial personality disorders with no co-occurring disorders. These clients are generally very verbal and aggressive. If placed in a heterogeneous group they would most likely violate the group boundaries and members in the group. Clients with antisocial personality disorders need well-trained and experienced therapists that are capable of placing significant limits on the client's behaviors within the group.
3. Clients diagnosed with antisocial personality disorder and a substance abuse disorder.
4. Clients diagnosed with a substance abuse disorder only.
5. Clients referred for sexual offending. Criminal justice clients should be separated by diagnosis because it not only lets the therapist know what they can expect from the client during the group treatment process, but also the group goals will be

> different. Obviously, a group made up of all antisocial personality disorders and antisocial personality disorders with substance abuse problems will present more formidable challenges to the therapist than a group of clients diagnosed with a primary substance abuse disorder only. The advantages of establishing groups that are uniform in composition is that the members can see that others have similar problems to theirs, it increases acceptance of each other, members are more willing to confront each other, members are more willing to utilize self-disclosure, and group members are more empathetic which increases the effectiveness of the group.

Many counselors conducting criminal justice groups believe that heterogeneity is helpful because clients with the least severe problems will learn from the clients with more severe problems.

(Friedman, 1989) in his work Practical Group Therapy, states "generally, a group will move as fast as its sickest member will permit. Hence, it is important to have as much homogeneity as possible with respect to level of pathology." Establishing homogeneous offender groups is also important because of the characteristics the clients have in common. Most times criminal justice offender groups that are heterogeneous are not very effective because the clients' characteristics don't go well together. This is understandable because people are different. A substance abuser may have a difficult time understanding why an antisocial personality disorder would commit a crime if it was not for getting drugs, just as the antisocial personality disorder may have a difficult time understanding why the substance abuser steals only for drugs. Their characteristics are different.

Many times a poor match between the group and the client is not always identified immediately. Continued assessment will make certain that the client is in a group in which they can change their behaviors without having an undesirable effect on other group members. Therefore, part of the therapist's continuing assessment should not only be the client's ability to participate in group, but also how the client's participation affects the group as a whole. A client's lack of participation could have an undesirable effect on the group's ability to develop a sense of togetherness and cohesiveness.

When referred to counseling, most criminal justice clients seem to know each other. This is because they either know each other from the streets or they were in jail or detention with each other at one time or another. Generally, whether clients know each other is not discovered during the screening process, but becomes obvious when they are introduced to the group. This can create some special problems relating to group confidentiality as well as how the clients knowing each other can effect their interactions within the group. If this situation does occur, and it most likely will, the therapist needs to determine, either within the group or by having an individual session with each client, the degree they think their knowing each other will prevent them from fully participating in group. If the therapist makes the decision after interviewing the clients to allow the new member in group it will be important for the therapist to continue assessing the appropriateness of the clients being in the same group together. If it appears during the therapist's continued assessment that the clients knowing each other is interfering with their participation, the new client should be transferred to another group.

Ethnic and Cultural Considerations

Clients referred from the criminal justice system represent a wide range of racial and cultural populations that could create problems in group treatment if they don't meet the present admission criteria, or if there is no criteria to determine the eligibility of a culturally different client. Admission issues are generally straightforward for most referrals. In the case of a culturally different client cultural, social and religious influences must be assessed. The therapist will need to decide after careful assessment if they have the skills to work effectively with the client's cultural beliefs, or if they are so different and the client is prone to expressing their cultural beliefs and opinions that they would be better served being referred elsewhere. If the therapist decides to accept the client, the therapist should first see the client in individual sessions where they can learn about their culture, develop trust, rapport and a therapeutic alliance with them. The individual meeting assists with the client's adjustment making it easier to transfer them into group therapy.

Stereotypes and ignorance about a client who is of a different race or culture could result in fear and further isolation of that client from the other group members. Group members, as well as therapists, sometimes lack knowledge and education about minority cultures. Because there are so many minorities referred by the criminal justice system for assessment and counseling services therapists need to establish group norms that take into consideration ethnic and cultural variables and values. The successful integration of minorities into a group therapy setting cannot occur until the group norms have been corrected and put into action. However, this cannot occur unless the therapist is first educated about the values and lifestyles of the minorities they are treating. This is a basic requirement when treating a minority in order to distinguish the difference between which thoughts, feelings and behaviors are characteristics of the client's culture and which are psychopathological.

Some suggestions to provide the kind of values that can foster cultural competency within groups include:

1. Teach group members that family characteristics are different in various cultures of the clients in the group.
2. Understand that shame associated with mental health services and the perception of being psychologically healthy varies from culture to culture.
3. Understand and accept that the therapist's and the group's moral beliefs may be different than the culturally different group member.
4. Accept that male and female roles within minority families may vary from culture to culture.
5. Recognize that your culturally different client may not desire to fully assimilate into the mainstream culture in fear of losing their own cultural identity.
6. Confront group members when they are engaging in language or behaviors that are culturally insensitive, prejudice, or discriminatory and assist them to understand how such language or behaviors harm others.
7. Avoid imposing beliefs, morals and values that may

be in disagreement with group members of a different culture.
8. Recognize that religious beliefs may influence the client's reaction and approach to their participation in group therapy.
9. Review current research that is related to the lack of quality in ethnic and racial mental health services.

It is extremely important that the therapist figure out ways to make changes to the strategies utilized in order to meet the varied needs of a culturally heterogeneous group of criminal justice clients. Many times our techniques and interventions are a mirror image of our own rules, values and beliefs without us even recognizing it. Being aware and changing group strategies as well as being culturally sensitive will improve the probability of the minority group member relating to the therapist and the group as a whole, and thereby increase treatment effectiveness for the client. Trust is almost always an issue for the culturally different criminal justice client. Trust can be developed by the therapist being culturally sensitive, not just between the therapist and the culturally different member, but also among other group members.

If you are contemplating opening a clinic to serve criminal justice clients, whether you receive clients that are culturally different is generally determined by the clinics' location. Culturally heterogeneous groups have been my preference because they accurately reflect community cultural demographics and provide the opportunity to identify the interpersonal conflicts between criminal justice clients from different racial and cultural backgrounds.

Specialized Training

Training and education is essential for mental health professionals wanting to specialize in the treatment of general offenders, sex offenders and substance abusers that are referred from the criminal justice and correctional system. Competencies in substance abuse treatment, sexual offending dynamics, criminal behavior, and criminal justice procedures are required in order to be effective. Training in these areas will help lessen the mistakes most beginning forensic counselors make. The most common mistake made by beginning forensic counselors is under estimating the criminal justice client's ability to sabotage any attempts to assist them in changing their criminal attitudes and lifestyles. This is because they are street wise and very skillful at figuring out what the therapist is doing, sabotaging the intervention and in so doing making a fool of the therapist. Some of the mistakes beginning forensic counselors make include:

1. Not screening clients as to their appropriateness for group therapy.
2. Not educating the client about group therapy prior to placing them in group.
3. Trying to do individual therapy instead of utilizing the group's dynamics.
4. Not establishing group norms.
5. Not establishing rules and expectations.
6. Not recognizing and resolving transference and counter-transference issues.
7. Trying to relate to the client by using street language.

8. Doing favors for the client.
9. Not recognizing that the client is qualifying their answer to an intervention with "maybe," "could be," "probably" or "possibly" instead of a "yes" or "no" as should be required.
10. Allowing clients to not complete assignments.
11. Not providing the group with structure.
12. Using a non-directive instead of a directive counseling approach.
13. Establishing groups without goals or a mission.

Cross training in substance abuse treatment, sexual offending, criminal behavior and criminal justice procedures is critical because:

1. Criminal offending in most cases is both a criminal justice and mental health issue requiring cross knowledge.
2. The increasing need for general practitioners in the mental health profession.
3. The increasing arrest and conviction rates of offenders that are referred for community treatment services by the courts in lieu of incarceration.

Group therapy is considered "best practice" for treating general offenders, sex offenders and substance abusers with a focus on:

1. Protection of the community.
2. Cognitive restructuring of thoughts, beliefs and feelings.

3. Social skills development.
4. Empathy training.
5. Developing a pro-social lifestyle.
6. Identifying high risk factors that contribute to their criminal acting out behavior.
7. Relapse prevention planning.
8. Complete disclosure of all offending.
9. Development of relationship skills.
10. Development of affective skills.
11. Identification of offending patterns or cycles.
12. Arousal control in sex offender treatment groups only.

The effective group therapist working with the criminal justice population will need training in a wide range of counseling theories because:

1. The client's determination to figure out what the therapist is doing so it can be sabotaged.
2. Not all clients respond to the same counseling approach.

Cognitive-behavioral therapy (CBT) is considered to be the "best practice" approach to treating a variety of criminal justice offenses and populations, however, some clients do not respond to CBT approaches but may respond better to transactional analysis, a psychodynamic approach or reality therapy. My recommendation to beginning forensic counselors is to become familiar with and trained in not just CBT, but also in other therapies that also work well with offenders such as reality therapy and transactional analysis. As a practical matter, the more tools you have to work with, the more effective you can be.

Clinical Supervision

In my clinical experience, the training of group therapists in most agencies has generally consisted of a few didactic workshops, sitting in on a few group therapy sessions as a co-therapist or just viewing a few videotapes. The training for group therapists in most agencies is insufficient because group therapists that are trained in such a manner are not very effective in achieving group goals and believe that their individual therapy skills will also work in group therapy. Many are also expected to figure out the training and experience they will need to run a group on their own.

Training in group process, group dynamics and group therapy theory can include didactic workshops, but it should also include:

1. Experiential learning such as participating in a training group with a well trained therapist.
2. Participating in a personal therapy group.
3. Attending annual conferences offering group therapy training such as those offered by the American Group Psychotherapy Association or the National Association of Forensic Counselors.

An important part of group therapy training is supervision of your work in group by an experienced group therapist. Supervision should be conducted in a supervisory group setting. This type of setting allows the beginning group therapist to gain experience and assists them in understanding exactly what is going on in the group which encourages formal discussion about theory, process, techniques and group dynamics. This type of supervision will assist the beginning group therapist in developing competent group skills and will improve their therapeutic effectiveness that will make possible changes in the criminal justice clients that are in their group.

Since group therapy with criminal justice clients differs from doing groups with other mental health populations the group therapy supervisor should possess the skills and knowledge themselves to evaluate the various competencies that the forensic group therapy trainee is required to become skilled in. These supervisor competencies include:

1. Knowledge of the psychodynamics of criminal behavior.
2. Knowledge of substance abuse.
3. Knowledge of sexual offending dynamics.
4. Knowledge of group dynamic theory.
5. Knowledge of common co-morbid psychiatric disorders.
6. Knowledge of group developmental stages.
7. Knowledge of various theoretical approaches.
8. Knowledge of supervision procedures that are followed during the course of training.
9. Knowledge of group process.
10. Knowledge of group techniques.

A competent group therapy supervisor must also, prior to providing the training and supervision, take into account the characteristics of the trainee, such as their motivation, commitment to supervision and their ability to acquire the required knowledge and skills to work with criminal justice clients.

There are other approaches to group therapy supervision

that are less effective because of the type of population with which we work. The group skills that are required in order to be effective with these clients is difficult to obtain from dyadic, video and audio types of supervision because it creates a sense of isolation and anxiety for the new trainee as opposed to a sense of belonging. Supervision must be from a well-trained, experienced forensic group counselor that understands the special needs and group dynamics that occur with criminal justice clients in a group therapy setting. The clinical function that the supervisor performs is the advancement of knowledge and skills, which in the case of the criminal justice client must include a thorough understanding of the elements and psychodynamics of criminal behavior, sexual offending, substance abuse, group process, group dynamics and stages of group development. The relationship between the trainee and their supervisor must be a supportive one. Once the new group therapist begins to utilize their newly learned skills they will need support, as well as feedback, from a perceptive supervisor. A positive supervisory alliance is important in order to have a constructive working relationship between supervisor and trainee in order for the trainee to learn the knowledge and skills that will be required for them to lead a group. Developing group competencies is an ongoing process and does not end after preliminary training and supervision. Continuing education to keep abreast of technological changes, therapy developments, changes in mental health delivery systems, criminal justice clients' needs and ethics is also required.

Chapter 2: Client Screening and Group Assignment

Referrals to Group Therapy

(Klein 1983) in his article published in the International Journal of Group Therapy entitled, "Some problems of patient referral for outpatient group therapy" he noted that comparatively little has been written about ensuring enough appropriate referrals for one's group. Non-violent criminal justice client referrals have greatly increased during the past several years primarily because of the prison over crowding problems and recognition by the criminal justice system that most offenders can be treated in the community. However, making certain that these referrals are appropriate for outpatient group therapy is critical and no less a concern for the group therapist specializing in treating criminal justice clients, because appropriate clients are the life source of their group as well as their private practice, program or agency.

Creating a program or a therapy group for criminal justice clients that will be both effective for the client as well as the referral source is a multifaceted responsibility requiring cooperation between the group therapist, the agency and the criminal justice referral source. Cooperation between these parties is critical for the success of the therapy group for the referred clients.

The biggest problem most group therapists experience accepting referrals from the criminal justice system is that the referring judge or probation officer believes that every offender is suitable for group treatment. If the therapist is dependent on the criminal justice system for referrals, this problem can most times be easily resolved by:

1. Educating the referral source on the importance of having group admission criteria.
2. Educating the referral source on group client screening and selection procedures and its importance for the other group members.
3. Educating the referral source to the other types of groups that may have a psychoeducational task, focus groups, or individual therapy to which a client that does not meet the criteria for group therapy may be assigned.
4. Educate the referral source about group rules and reasons a client may be terminated and refer them back as unsuccessfully completing the program.
5. Informing the referral source as to the group's goals and/or mission.
6. Writing up a referral agreement between the agency and the referring court or probation department clearly delineating the services that will be provided.

Taking the time to educate the referral source is a good investment of your time. Be certain that you stress the point that a referral to you is not a direct admission into your group or program. Be clear that the client must be assessed and screened as to their appropriateness to be accepted in group therapy. If the client is found not appropriate they may be admitted into a different type of group within your agency or program or referred to another agency that can better meet the needs of the client. By investing your time and energy to be thorough about your group criteria and screening procedures with your referral source demonstrates your professionalism as a competent group therapist who is effective and knows and understands the psychodynamics of criminal justice clients and criminal behavior. In my experience, taking this time is appreciated by the referral source and results in a steady flow of clients for assessments and group admission screening for the life of the program or group.

The Intake Interview

The referral from the court brings the client to their intake interview. Client intake procedures seem to differ from agency to agency; however, the general formats have some similarities. The client is generally required to complete their intake interview and paperwork which generally includes:

1. Demographic information such as name, address, marital status, number of children, level of education, place of employment, occupation and emergency contact.
2. Medical history.
3. Financial agreement.
4. Informed consent form.
5. Releases of information.
6. Psychosocial history.

The client, during their intake interview, is advised of the limited confidentiality and what information must be released to the court or probation department. The client either agrees or disagrees to the limited confidentiality. If the client disagrees and refuses to sign the informed consent form and releases of information they are referred back to the court or probation department that referred them. If they agree, they are then scheduled for a diagnostic interview with a therapist who will discuss the client's treatment needs. Generally, the therapist who referred the client for group therapy does the diagnostic evaluation and treatment planning with the client. I have observed quite a few criminal justice counseling programs where the intake worker assigns the client to a group. This procedure is inappropriate and could result in poorly composed groups that are extremely disorganized and lack any therapeutic efficacy.

The Screening Interview

In my experience, clients referred from the criminal justice system are generally resistant to the suggestion that they participate in group therapy, or for that matter that they participate in any type of counseling which indicates their lack of willingness and motivation. They generally respond with outright denial of their need for counseling or participation in group therapy, giving reasons such as "I don't need counseling," "I don't have any problems," or "I was in group therapy before and it doesn't work." In most offender programs the therapist at this point becomes confrontational which seldom, if ever, works out well. Instead of confrontation, it is more productive to utilize motivational interviewing techniques as presented by (Miller and Rollnick, 1995) to overcome the client's resistance. Going with the client's resistance by allowing them to verbalize their feelings about being forced into treatment, without the therapist being critical, can be the basis for developing rapport and trust because this is probably the first time someone is willing to listen to their complaints. The therapist should be sensitive to the client's complaints as well as their fears and anxieties about being in a group. This provides the opportunity to explore with the client their here-and-now fears that are contributing to their resistance and lack of motivation. Next, find out the client's expectations for group screening, their understanding of the process, as well as why they were referred to you. Some useful questions that may assist in lowering the client's resistance and assist in determining if the client is appropriate for group may include:

1. "What happened that resulted in your being referred here?"
2. "How do you feel about being sent here?"
3. "What were you aware of as you were coming here for your appointment with me?"
4. "Where would you rather be, here or speaking with your probation officer?"
5. "What do you think will happen if you choose not to participate in treatment?"
6. "If you decide that you will participate in group, what would you most want to change?"
7. "What are you feeling right now that is a concern to you?"
8. "If you had a perfect life, what would it be?"
9. "What would you be willing to do to get a better life?"

10. "What fears do you have about attending group therapy?"
11. "Do you think that being arrested and convicted of a crime(s) may indicate that you have a problem?"
12. "How do you think your arrest and conviction affected your family and others?"
13. "If you could change those behaviors that caused you to be arrested, how would you do that?"

The next step is to determine if the client's diagnosis is appropriate for your group. If you are forming a homogeneous group as recommended, the diagnosis is important. The diagnosis assists in determining what behaviors we can expect, as well as what the client's response to treatment may be, and the probability of the client successfully completing the program. During the screening interview, based on your clinical observations, you should be able to determine with some accuracy what to expect from the client if you accept them into your group or program.

If a client is found to be appropriate for group therapy and has agreed to participate, the next step is the development of a problem-oriented treatment plan. By developing the treatment plan prior to the client entering your group, the client will better understand what is expected from them and increase the probability of therapeutic efficacy.

It is important to remember that when developing the treatment plan that specific interpersonal problems be identified as well as any problems that may directly relate to or be connected to the crime(s) the client was referred for such as substance abuse, family problems, unemployment, poor living environment, distorted thinking, poor attitude or other reasons.

It takes considerable skill to identify the criminal justice client's real problems, because they are mandated to attend treatment and they are most likely being compliant in order to avoid any further consequences. Therefore, the answers you initially receive may not be very useful at all. The problems identified should be as close to what the client's official records indicate they are such as in:

1. Police reports.
2. Previous treatment records.
3. Victim statements.
4. Court records.
5. Previous probation supervision reports.
6. Presentence interview (PSI).
7. Medical records.
8. Psychiatric reports.
9. Family/significant other interviews.
10. Employment history record.

To assure an accurate identification of the client's life problems requires that you become fully aware of the client's history by reviewing available records. In this manner you are able to confront any incongruency between what the client tells you and the official record. This process takes patience and probing skills on the part of the therapist, but results most times in an accurate identification of the client's problems.

Preparing the Client for Group

Assuming that the client has agreed to participate in your group and the treatment plan has been developed, the next step is to prepare the client for entry into the group. The purpose of client preparation is to let the client know how to participate in a group, group rules, and group expectations. There are several different formats that can be utilized to prepare clients for entry into a group. One method is to meet with the client individually if you already have an existing group. The other method you can use if you are starting a new group is to meet with the group candidates in a classroom setting. With either format, the information to be shared with the client is the same. It is important to be clear in your presentation to the client so they don't become confused or anxious. Most criminal justice clients generally don't ask questions because they are trying to be compliant with the court mandate that they attend treatment. If they do ask a question it is usually a general question without much practical value or importance. At this point, the burden falls upon the therapist to have each client oriented to explain what they heard in detail and what thoughts and feelings they are experiencing. In most programs serving criminal justice clients, resources are fairly limited and only one orientation session is available. One session should be sufficient if the therapist covers all the materials thoroughly.

The orientation session is an instructional function which requires the instructing therapist to have available materials such as group therapy brochures, videos, agency and group rules as well as other materials that will assist the client to prepare for group. This instructional format serves the purpose of ensuring that the client understands the group's mission or goals and expectations, and if they are willing to accept them, as well as assisting the client in understanding how group therapy works.

The orientation session should cover at a minimum:

1. Group mission or goals.
2. Client's goals.
3. Group contract.
4. Group rules.
5. Termination for rule violations and the possible consequences.
6. How to participate in the group.
7. Attendance expectations and consequences for not attending.
8. Behaviors that are unacceptable which may present an obstacle to group work.
9. That treatment may be a long-term process.
10. Group confidentiality.
11. Client fees.

Most therapists are reluctant to discuss fees with their clients. Discussion of fees is important with criminal justice clients because they have been traditionally unreliable in paying their debts which has contributed in part to their present life situation. It is important that they fully understand that they are responsible for their fees as arranged with the intake worker. If you fail to emphasize this point you can be assured they will not pay their required fee. In fact, (Rutan and Stone, 1984) regard fee issues as a group issue. If the client becomes irresponsible in paying their fees, this issue can be discussed in group.

It has always proven effective for me to take the time to

fully explain the importance of the group contract to the possible new member. The group contract clearly delineates the expectations, as well as the standards and conduct, that is required from the group and the group therapist. For example, the group contract should stipulate where group sessions will be held and at what time they will begin and end. The contract should also require a commitment by the client that once they enter the group they commit to attending for a specific period of time. During my orientations, I advise all possible new group members that at least one year will be required. This sometimes causes the client to verbalize their unhappiness; however, I take the time to review with the client all their life problems, and let them know up front that there are no short short-term solutions for their long-term antisocial behaviors and life problems they caused. The contract needs to be very specific and presented to the client not just as a program formality, but also as something that should be taken into serious consideration. This generally de-escalates the client's discomfort and gains their cooperation. Being honest and up front with the client also works in establishing trust and a positive therapeutic alliance. Appendix A contains a sample group contract that may be used as is or modified to meet your or the group's needs.

The majority of criminal justice clients resist sharing anything personal unless they feel safe that they can trust the therapist and the group as a whole. This can be quite a task for even a trained and experienced therapist. One way to develop and establish trust with this difficult client population is to clearly define during their pre-group orientation exactly what group confidentiality is and the consequences for violating the group's confidentiality. Even after the new member enters your group it is important to remind the whole group at the beginning of each session the importance of confidentiality. Remind group members that it is okay to discuss what they have learned outside of group what they have learned, or how they have benefited from participating in the group but under no circumstances can they share the identity of other group members. The pre-group orientation is also a good time to again discuss with the client the limitations of confidentiality and what can be shared with whom and why.

Brief the client on what they may possibly get out of group. There are a few things that you can do during the pre-group orientation that can maximize the possibility for the client that is going to enter a group to help make sure that the experience will be a meaningful and healing experience for them by informing them:

1. The more they participate and commit to the group, the more they and the group will benefit by achieving the group's mission.
2. Talk about themselves and their problems in group and ask group members for feedback.
3. Be honest in group. The more honest they are the more they can be helped.
4. Focus on their treatment plan, which is their road map to recovery.
5. Express their thoughts and feelings with other group members.
6. Don't share anything that makes them uncomfortable.
7. Confront other group members when they sense they are being dishonest or unreal.
8. Try out new behaviors in group and seek out

feedback.

9. Provide feedback to other group members so they understand how they may be perceived by others.

There may be other benefits that are specific to your groups that you may want to share with the client on how group therapy may assist them in their recovery and how they need to actively participate to be helped. Talking with the client will help lower some of their anxiety and unrealistic expectations.

A strong emphasis should be placed on the importance of the client's attendance in group even though it may at times be difficult or upsetting to them. The client should be made aware that by being determined and committed to their treatment they can recover and return to a pro-social lifestyle. The first three months in treatment for the criminal justice client are critical. It is during the first three months that the client is at risk of terminating or dropping out of treatment and returning to their previous lifestyles. Client retention rates are greatly improved by preparing the client to enter a group and their commitment to the process during the early stages of group treatment. (Yalom 1995, p. 315) wrote that premature termination generally "stems from problems caused by deviancy, sub-grouping, conflicts in intimacy and disclosure, the role of the early provocateur, external stress, complications of concurrent individual and group therapy, inability to share the leader, inadequate preparation, and emotional contagion."

When using either method for preparing a client for entry into a group, it is best that the group therapist do the orientation rather than the intake worker. If you are working with a co-therapist both of you should attend the orientation session together. This allows the client to meet their therapist which could become the beginning of a positive therapeutic alliance. This procedure allows both the therapist and co-therapist to discuss their impressions of each client, what they may expect from the client(s), and to identify early any possible counter-transference issues that may need to be resolved prior to a client entering the group.

Introducing the New Client to the Group

Practices on how to inform group members that a new member is entering the group vary significantly depending upon the setting and type of group. Some therapists inform their groups that a new member is coming several weeks in advance and don't give any specific details. Other therapists tell the member's age and charge. Other therapists seek the group's permission to allow a new member into the group. I personally don't tell the group know anything. My groups find out that a new member is joining the group when the new member first gets to the group. In my experience as a group therapist specializing in working with criminal justice clients, I have found that the group was not concerned about who was entering the group and any information that was shared with them was forgotten by the time the new member came into the group. Group members know without reservation in an open-ended group that when a member is terminated a new member will be taking their place. I personally believe that it is a waste of valuable group time to seek permission or discuss in advance the entry of a new member to the group. Possibly with other types of populations it would be important, however, for the most part we are working with a group that has the attitude that everything is BS and nothing is real. In a criminal justice client group, all the members have been mandated by the court of jurisdiction to attend treatment. Mandating treatment is non-conforming to the traditional practice of client referral to treatment for many reasons including the lack of a voluntary informed consent which creates an asymmetrical therapist-client relationship in a number of areas. In court-mandated programs and groups, the therapist must be the group leader rather than a facilitator, directive rather than nondirective, therefore wasting group time weeks in advance discussing a new member's group entry or seeking permission to allow a new member to enter group is not suggested. Seeking the group's permission to admit a new member to the group could also destabilize the group leader's position as the group leader.

The manner in which a new client is introduced to a group depends largely on the type of group and whether the group is open ended or closed. In the present case we are discussing open-ended groups for offenders where members come and go, so it is essential that new members be introduced.

When introducing a new member to group, keep it simple. First, have the new member introduce themselves and the reason they are in group, and then have the group members introduce themselves by first name and a short statement about why they are in group. Try to avoid going around the group circle as it is usually done which enables each group member the opportunity to take responsibility for themselves. This allows each group member to be spontaneous and allows each group member to think about how the group has been helping them. Examples of some methods that you can use to get the introductions started include:

1. "Would you introduce yourself to the group, and a brief statement about what brought you here and what you expect to get from being here?"
2. "Who would like to introduce themselves to our new group member with a brief statement of why you are here and how you think you have benefited from being in group?"

Chapter 3: Group Development

There are numerous theories on group development which do not apply specifically to criminal justice populations. Group therapy is considered to be best practice for treating criminal offenders, however, whether it is effective or not is dependent upon the therapist's training and experience. Some offender groups are based upon the clinical experience of the therapist and have no empirical base to them and at best are barely on the fringe of appropriateness, if not just outright ineffective.

The historical approach to offender group therapy has been to utilize high confrontation techniques that are believed to break down the offender's denial system; however, such approaches have only worked in getting the client that is being confronted to adapt to whatever the therapist wanted to hear. The client quickly figured out what the therapist was doing and wanted, and responded accordingly. In other words, this approach has not been very effective in assisting the client to think through an intervention and then reply in a genuine manner. In fact, according to (Yalom, 1995) "therapeutic groups can directly contribute to adverse outcomes for some clients, including the experience of enduring psychological distress attributable to one's group experience." My observation of programs that utilize high confrontation techniques is that they also have very high drop out rates and contribute to lowered self-esteem of clients that are not only vulnerable because they are mandated to attend, but they already suffer from low self-esteem and poor self image, as well as the possibility of antisocial acting out behaviors outside of the group setting. In most treatment settings, including substance abuse groups, high confrontation has not been demonstrated to be effective.

Not every criminal justice client is going to benefit from being in group therapy; however, every therapist that has chosen to specialize in the treatment of offenders should provide quality treatment that will contribute to the client achieving their therapeutic goals and reduce the risk of adverse consequences. High confrontation techniques are quantity not quality, and in many cases contribute to the possibility of an adverse outcome for those clients participating in such a group. Evaluating each group member's progress or lack of progress while in a therapeutic group can assist the therapist in identifying possible adverse outcomes and provides the opportunity to modify treatment approaches as may be needed that are consistent with the client's needs and progress. Ongoing evaluation of the group member's progress will result in a substantial reduction in adverse outcomes.

Confrontation is a legitimate form of intervention when it is used to point out inconsistencies rather than attacking the client. Simply making the client aware of what they are saying and how it may be inconsistent with reality is sufficient. That is therapeutic confrontation and has little or no risk of harming the therapeutic alliance or causing an adverse treatment outcome.

Why Group Therapy?

Group therapy is considered to be best practice for the treatment of most, but not all, criminal justice clients. Criminal justice clients with a diagnosis of antisocial personality disorder, substance abuse disorder, domestic violence batterers or sexual offending disorders are appropriate for group therapy if they meet the ideal client criteria discussed in the previous chapter. There are a number of reasons why group therapy is considered to be best practice with criminal justice offenders, such as:

1. Group brings together individuals with common problems.
2. Group members with common problems may express empathy with each other.
3. Group provides a safe place for members to speak candidly about their crimes, lifestyle, feelings, concerns and views.
4. Group members provide and receive feedback from each other.
5. It is more difficult to lie, cheat, con and manipulate in group.
6. Issues raised in group evoke different viewpoints from members.
7. Group members learn interpersonal skills easier in a group setting.
8. Group members learn alternative ways of thinking,

feeling and behaving.
9. Group members learn how to resolve problems and conflicts easier in a group setting.
10. Group reduces the offender's sense of isolation and abandonment.
11. Group members provide support in the recovery process.
12. Group members support each other in not re-offending.
13. Group therapy can encourage hope and determination.

The group process puts forward the probability that the group member's life experiences and issues experienced in their daily lives will surface in the group dynamic. For example, a group member that easily becomes angry will most likely become angry in group. A group member that has problems with authority and authority figures will very likely have problems with the therapist and being confronted by other group members in the group.

The group process also allocates some group time to process group member's feedback and comments in order to understand and work effectively with group member's relationships with each other. Many times transference and counter-transference issues arise in groups where the client may project what is going on with another group member in the present with a relationship or experience in the past. For example, when a group member relates that Jerry reminds him of his father, or another group member confronts Jerry with not liking him just like everyone else he knows. The following are some examples of process comments that should be processed in group:

"I really like Jerry because we have a lot in common with each other. Jerry reminds me of my father, because we never got along with each other and he was abusive."

"Jerry, I don't think you're being honest in group. I think your still conning."

"Jerry, you just don't understand my problem."

"Jerry, I think you don't like me very much just like everyone else I know."

Members may remind each other of others in their past or present which brings forth thoughts and feelings. By engaging with one another on different emotional levels, group members may hopefully gain a different perspective about the ways their internal frame of reference is reflected in their relationships with each other and society as a whole. As each group member gains awareness they also begin to identify new characteristics about themselves. A very common phenomenon among criminal justice clients within a group setting is how hard they will work not to become aware of various emotional aspects of themselves in order to avoid painful thoughts, memories and feelings. It is within the safe, supportive group experience that a criminal justice client can recognize and acknowledge their contaminated thoughts, feelings, beliefs and behaviors and replace them with pro-social and uncontaminated choices that can resolve their emotional conflicts and social problems with feelings of confidence and self-esteem.

Group therapy for criminal justice offenders has many more benefits for this population that has previously been labeled as being untreatable. Many offenders have had difficult, if not traumatizing, experiences attempting to live a pro-social lifestyle, particularly with groups and individuals that place barriers to their recovery. Group can offer them different experiences with each member supporting recovery that can work to heal those past attempts to block recovery. Emphasizing support, expressing feelings, safety, trust and encouragement to overcome their barriers to recovery are all powerful ways to address their stigmization as offenders. The group experience should challenge them to examine their distorted thoughts, beliefs, feelings and antisocial lifestyle patterns that inhibit them. Encourage the client to use their toughness and energy to overcome their barriers to recovery in a pro-social way. Also, remind the client that "when the going gets tough, the tough get going," which means they must persist in spite of attempts to hold them back.

The experience of most criminal justice offender's is that the system has set them up and left them feeling abandoned, isolated, dismissed, rejected and inferior because of their conviction. These experiences can and do re-create the very same problems they encountered as a child that resulted in the development of their antisocial frames of reference. Group therapy provides a very powerful therapeutic benefit for those criminal justice offenders that are willing to actively participate and undertake the challenge to utilize the group for its intended purpose.

Group Size

The preference for group size seems to vary considerably throughout the literature as well as with therapists. When working with criminal justice clients in a group setting my recommendation has always been 8-12 clients. I, myself, personally prefer to have no more than 12 clients in my group and will not accept a new member until there is an opening to the group. I have seen substance abuse groups and offender groups that have as many as 20-25 members in them because of either insufficiently trained staff or a shortage of funding. Large groups are ineffective because they encourage hiding out and doing nothing, create chaos and prevent a true therapeutic alliance. Large groups are not supportive of a successful treatment outcome and many times results in an adverse outcome.

The advantages of a small (8-12) member open-ended criminal justice client group are:

1. Therapist and group members know each other.
2. Group membership is fixed allowing new members only when openings occur.
3. Group members know how the group operates.
4. The group is structured and controllable.
5. Group cohesion is more easily developed.
6. The therapist can more easily manage and identify issues that may need to be addressed during each of the group's developmental stages.
7. Conflict and resolution processes may be addressed more effectively.
8. Easier for new members to adjust to the group.
9. More time for clients to work and participate.
10. Easier to allocate time for group processing.
11. The group develops and provides a counter culture to the criminal justice client's subculture lifestyle.
12. Group rules are better adhered.
13. Difficult for clients to maintain secrets about outside activities.

14. Group members become more willing to utilize self-disclosure.
15. Group members become more willing to confront each other.

Keeping the group size small, with no more than 8-12 members, encourages participation and is easier for group members to learn. Group members feel as though they are being listened to and understood by other group members as they begin to develop a sense of being connected and part of the group. This is impossible in large groups of 20-25 members.

Group Cohesion

Whether a criminal justice client group develops cohesiveness or not is dependent upon a variety of factors that may interfere with or contribute to the group's early stages of development. The appropriate screening of clients prior to entering a group is necessary to eliminate those that present an obvious deterrent to the development of group cohesiveness. Appropriate screening is critical to the group's success or failure. Items to think about when screening a client are the following:

1. The abilities of clients selected to actively participate.
2. The client's personality characteristics.
3. Client's motivation.
4. The group's goals or mission.
5. Group size.
6. Duration of the group.

7. The training, skills and experience of the group therapist.

Under the factors listed as the client's ability, personality characteristics and motivation it is quite common for groups consisting of only criminal justice offenders during the early stages of the group's development to demonstrate high levels of resistance to change, be distrustful of others, and to have conflicts with other group members and the group therapist. These issues are considered to be part of the personality characteristics of most criminal justice offenders. These personality characteristics are issues that are generally dealt with and resolved during a group's early stages of development. However, when clients frequently drop out during a group's early stages of development it creates severe problems in resolving the intrinsic issues that must be resolved in order for the group to progress to its next stage of development. Therefore, it is important that the client, prior to being admitted into the group, be properly screened as to their ability to actively participate and their level of motivation to change. If the client does not own their present offense for which they have been referred to treatment for, and indicates that they don't want to participate in a group, they should not be admitted into a group. Admitting inappropriate clients into a group that present a high risk of dropping out only deters the development of a climate of trust and cohesiveness the group must achieve in order fulfill its mission. A group is more likely to achieve its goal or mission efficiently if the group's membership consists of stable and appropriate members.

Another factor contributing to the successful development

of cohesiveness is the size of the group. As previously stated, the optimum size of a group is about 8-12 members. When there are more than 12 members in a group communication becomes unclear and can create an environment of hiding out and doing nothing which hinders the development of cohesiveness.

The duration of a group also plays a critical role in the development of trust and cohesiveness. An open-ended criminal justice client psychotherapy group is more likely to be successful in realizing its mission than a closed group, primarily because of the client's intrinsic personality characteristics and deeply ingrained pathologies that require time to explore and restructure. This can only occur in a group that has developed a high level of trust among its members and achieved the group goal of cohesiveness.

Group Developmental Stages

Starting a new group from scratch is a lot of responsibility and hard work for a therapist who must have the training, skills, knowledge and experience necessary to assure the group's success. When a new group begins it is normal for group members to experience anxiety and other discomforts primarily because they are unfamiliar with the therapist and each other. However, as a new group develops and group members become more familiar with the process their feelings and behaviors change. These changes will correlate with the stage of development the group is in. As previously discussed, the basic needs and requirements of starting a criminal justice client group are as follows:

1. Deciding on what type of group: open ended, closed, time limited, etc.
2. Defining the group's goal or mission.
3. Developing ideal client admission criteria.
4. Screening possible group candidates for group therapy.
5. Orientating group candidates prior to entering the group.
6. Introducing a new client into the group.

The various stages of group development are very similar to the development of a child from birth to adulthood. Therapy groups change and evolve over time and as members leave and enter. Criminal justice client groups are really no different in this respect; however, the developmental stages and the intensity of the issues that must be worked through during each stage do differ considerably from most other therapeutic groups just as they do from child to child in their development and socialization.

There is an overabundance of models and theories available on group development with some having as many as nine stages of development and some with as few as two stages. My group therapy experience has been that criminal justice groups go through four very specific stages of development. Stage I is Trust vs. Mistrust, Stage II is Acceptance vs. Rejection, Stage III is Initiative vs. Uncertainty, and Stage IV is Success vs. Failure. Knowledge of group development will assist you in recognizing how members deal with the issues at hand during each stage. This allows the therapist to develop appropriate interventions to deal with the issues at hand. The group goes through a process in its development to becoming a group that is encouraging of each other in making behavioral changes. It is therefore beneficial for the group therapist to have a thorough understanding of group dynamics. A solid understanding of group dynamics by the therapist will give the therapist a better understanding of how their group is progressing as well as what they can do to facilitate a positive treatment outcome. My own personal belief is that in order for groups to work through the developmental stages successfully, the group must flow from one session to the other. In other words, it requires that the last session be connected to the present session like turning pages in a book. This requires that the therapist be well organized and methodical to assure that group therapy be seen by the client as a continuing process from session to session. Some suggestions that may assist you in keeping your group connected are:

1. At the end of each group session have the group review what they may have learned and how they may transfer what they have learned outside of the group. Reviewing what was learned in group improves the quality of communication making the group process more memorable and makes the learning outcomes more transferable outside of the group.
2. At the beginning of each group session have the group members reflect back what was learned in the last group session and how they applied what was learned outside the group. Throughout the reflection of the previous group session, group members can point to and discuss any difficulties they experienced in their implementing the new

> learned behaviors. This attention to reflecting can highlight any significant moments or issues that would have ordinarily been missed.

This simple review and reflection method increases the level of support for the group process and provides the group with a sense of continuity from session to session in a non-threatening way. It also encourages full group participation, assists in the development of trust among group members, and also in the development of group cohesiveness.

Stage I - Trust vs. Mistrust

It is extremely difficult to create a trusting therapeutic environment within a group of 8-12 members who suffer from matching pathologies concerning their relationships with other people. This is especially true when their frame of reference is "don't trust others," "don't get close," "be tough," "don't snitch," "the world sucks," and a variety of other sayings based upon their early life experiences with others and their decisions based upon those experiences.

During this first stage of the group's development the most important undertaking the therapist has is to take the necessary steps that are required to create a trusting and safe environment. Just as a developing child must be nurtured and taught right from wrong, so does a developing group. You can fully expect that your new group members will test out the group environment in order for them to figure out what is real and what they can and cannot get away with. Most clients, during this stage of development, will be doubtful as to how safe the group really is and not be very willing to take the risk of fully participating. The primary issue during this stage is how safe is it for the client to take the risk of sharing. Because of the safety and trust issues during the group's first stage of development very little group cohesiveness will be observed; however, group cohesion will gradually develop as the therapist:

1. Establishes boundaries, group rules and healthy group norms pertaining to the level of participation that is expected within the group by modeling the behaviors that are expected. The norms that should be encouraged and modeled by the therapist include honesty, appropriate self-disclosure, risk taking, attentive participation, acceptance of others, and nonjudgmental responding (Flores, 1997).
2. Teaches the members in the group the fundamentals of group process. The therapist during this stage of development should be active and supportive by encouraging honest exchanges amongst group members with a focus on the here-and-now issues. For example, the therapist could say: "You and Robert seem to have identical issues relating to trusting others. Would you be willing to share with us how they are similar?"
3. Deals openly with the group's concerns and questions regarding their safety and trust issues. It is important to get the group to feel connected and that they share similar problems with each other in order to develop trust and group cohesiveness. According to (Marziali et al, 1997) among the components of group cohesion are "connectedness of the group demonstrated by working toward a common goal, acceptance, support, and

identification with the group, affiliation, acceptance, and attractiveness of the group and engagement."

4. Teaches the group appropriate interpersonal skills in their relationship with each other within the group such as responding to each other, listening carefully to what others are saying as well as the use of appropriate language. The therapist should take extra care to not allow group members to become involved in shameful, degrading or threatening responses to each other.
5. Provides a structure within the group that encourages the development of trust and safety, keeping in mind that during stage I development, the group is not fully prepared to withstand extreme conflicts. Conflict during this phase is unavoidable so the therapist should encourage group members to minimize confronting each other and instead encourage interactions that avoid any type of aggressive response.
6. Continuously models therapeutic behaviors regardless of how difficult or frustrating the group.
7. At all time maintains professional decorum and doesn't attempt to relate as being one of the guys by using street language.
8. At all times is honest and open in their relationship with the group.
9. Is psychologically available for the group.
10. Is empathetic to the group member's past and present life problems.
11. Keeps group members focused on their treatment plans and does not allow them to deviate from their treatment plan goals and objectives in their

> attempts to sabotage their treatment and recovery. The therapist should strive to keep the focus on the client's treatment plan and at all times encourage the client to work through the many objectives in a timely manner as delineated within the treatment plan.

Trust and safety is the basic issue to be dealt with during this stage of the group's development. Understand that it is not easy for this particular population to just open up and share their lives or discuss the crimes they committed. During this stage of group development fully expect the client to be hesitant to share. My experience has been that most of the group members are overly anxious about just being in a group setting and have no idea about what to expect or what may happen. Some are worried or afraid of what will happen if they do confront someone in group and if they will be labeled a snitch, or if they share something about their past will they be rejected or ridiculed. Some worry that others may talk about them outside of the group or snitch on them to their supervising probation or parole agent or police. Many of the group members will have other major concerns such as: "Will this be worth it?" "How will my life be if I change?" "Can I really do what is expected from me?" "What if they find out I'm mentally ill?" "Is it really safe here?" "Do I speak or wait to be asked to speak?" and "What will these other people in group think of me if I share my secret life with them?" It can also be expected during this stage of group development that most, if not all, the group members are going to be resistant. After all, this is not a voluntary group where people seek out help for their life problems. This is an involuntary group where the client was told to attend or they will go to jail or prison instead. It's forced treatment. When you force anyone to do something it is perfectly in accordance with human nature to resist. However, it is important for the therapist to recognize and acknowledge resistance within the group and not ignore it. Just ignoring it and hoping it will resolve itself just doesn't work. If the therapist does not deal with the resistance openly when identified then they will have a dysfunctional, unworkable group. It is important to explore with the group the source of the group's or a member's resistance. The therapist should validate their resistance by accepting their honesty. One of the things I learned early in my career is that whenever I encounter a client that appears to be resistant I always ask myself this question: "What am I discounting about my client right now that is causing them to react this way?" The majority of the time I realize that I discount my client's fear of the unknown.

Encouraging resistant group members to explore their fears, concerns or anger about being in a therapy group most times resolves the problem and assists in the development of trust and group cohesion. Allow the clients to verbalize their anger about being forced to be in group therapy without interruption. Be genuine and respectful in your understanding and express empathy in a clear and unambiguous way. Being honest, dependable and respectful with the client and the group as a whole is the foundation for developing trust.

Be clear about your role as therapist and issues relating to confidentiality within the group and define for them clearly what limited confidentiality means. I always define limited confidentiality; however, I also let clients know that if they speak about past crimes or misdeeds which I ask them to, that they do not to state where, when or how they did something so they can understand my role is not to trap them and report something they did. It is important if treatment is going to be effective that clients have the freedom to share their secret lives and past things they have done while in treatment without fear.

Stage I of the group's development is hard work for the therapist, and it will be hard work for the group members. Group members must ultimately be given the responsibility for making their group a success. Providing them with the opportunities to make their group a success may be the first time anyone has trusted them to do something perceived as being important for others. However, they need to know exactly what they can do to make their group a successful one. Some tasks I give my group during its early stage of development that places responsibility on them and gives each member a sense of participation are:

1. To assist me in developing the group norms, rules and boundaries by providing feedback to me.
2. To be open in expressing their concerns, hopes and expectations of what they have about being in a group and from me as their therapist.
3. To express openly with the group their anger about being forced to attend.
4. To be respectful when being confronted or when providing feedback to another member.
5. To assist me in identifying their high-risk factors that may contribute to their criminal acting out behaviors.
6. To work with me and the group in assisting them in developing realistic countermeasures to their high-risk factors.

7. To be supportive of each other in beating the system by not re-offending and making the changes the system and others don't really believe they can make.
8. To identify their educational and vocational needs so they can be assisted in getting them met so that they may participate in meaningful employment.
9. To assist each other in identifying past and present social barriers that have been preventing them from living a pro-social lifestyle.
10. To openly and honestly express their thoughts and feelings to the therapist and each other within the group to interventions, confrontations and member feedback.
11. To be responsible and take responsibility for following their treatment plan goals and objectives.

During this stage of group development we are focusing on establishing a safe therapeutic environment and trust by getting to know each other, discussing fears, expectations, hopes, how to interact with each other, how to listen and respond, how to express their thoughts and feelings in the here and now, and teaching them what they need to do to make their group, each other and themselves a success.

I have been asked by other therapists on numerous occasions during my training sessions to estimate how long it takes to achieve group trust with a criminal justice population. The answer I always give is that it is dependent upon the training, skills and experience of the therapist as well as the level of motivation of the clients within the group. There is no time limit. For some groups it may take three months and others it may take six or eight months or for some it may be as little as one or two months. It depends upon a variety of variables. Therapeutic groups do evolve and eventually trust and cohesion is achieved – even within criminal justice groups.

Stage II - Acceptance vs. Rejection

Stage II of a criminal justice group can be very complex because a set of related thoughts, feelings and expectations that may have been repressed during Stage I surface and continue to influence the group's thoughts and behaviors. Issues overlapping from Stage I may be difficult to recognize and even more difficult for the therapist to understand and analyze without full cooperation and assistance from the group.

During Stage II group cohesiveness is high; however, it is still developing. The therapist can easily determine which clients during this stage feel accepted by the group by observing their interactions with other group members. Individual group members during this stage experience a sense of belonging, being valued by other group members, and a feeling of friendliness.

During Stage II careful and thoughtful attention should be on group process, which is how members interact within the group. During this stage therapeutic work is beginning to occur containing both content and process which is assisting in making therapeutic connections among group members. However, feelings of anxiety still exist as some group members struggle with their concerns about safety, trust and rejection by the group. Some members may continue to test the therapist and the group environment in order to determine if it is safe or not, and some will continue to struggle with taking risks.

Group members will struggle with power and control issues and there will be conflict and confrontation. Some group members may roll their eyes or just stare in response to another member's response, or side conversations may occur. These are stimuli that are generally not within the client's awareness that can create conflict that requires exploration and should not be ignored by the therapist and should be processed within the group. Through the group process the clients learn how to work through the issues of power, control and conflict instead of avoiding them.

As you may have noticed, many of the issues being dealt with during Stage II appear to overlap. (Gerald Corey, et al, 2000) states that "no arbitrary dividing lines exist between the phases of a group. In actual practice these phases merge with each other."

Corey means that even if a group does reach the stage of actual therapeutic work occurring, not all members are going to be at the same level of development within the group. This is similar to two small children being the same age, but one is slightly more advanced than the other. We will discuss in some detail the process of individual client change in a later chapter and why one client may be more advanced than another client in the same group. However, the following is what you will observe in your group as it continues to develop and evolve. Some members will be right on target, some slightly behind, and even some more advanced. Early developmental issues will continue to resurface and will need to be dealt with by the therapist as they are identified. During Stage II the therapist should:

1. Allocate group time to address and process with the group issues of safety, trust, and new conflicts

as they arise. Teach members that are having a conflict to deal with them openly.

2. Recognize that some clients will continue to resist group participation and that such resistance should not be defined as being negative, but rather as being a normal and healthy response to involuntary treatment. At this point, the therapist should continue working through the resistance by encouraging the client to verbalize their concerns and processing their fears with the group as a whole in order to move the group into a more advanced stage of development and a deeper level of trust. Resistance will resurface from time to time and should not be ignored.
3. Create a therapeutic environment for the group to openly deal with conflict and resistance by defining those issues as something that may affect the entire group's progress and should be resolved by the group and therapist together. By not defining the problem as just a therapist-client issue, but rather a whole group issue, other group members are encouraged to participate and it assists in the development of cohesiveness.
4. Continue to facilitate the expression of here and now reactions to what is occurring in the group.
5. Encourage group members to express their anxieties. Assist the client in reducing their anxiety by providing a safe group structure and having a positive attitude, demonstrating positive regard and warmth in a convincing manner. The therapist should acknowledge the client and group when they achieve a goal or resolve group issues.

6. Deal openly and honestly with any and all challenges directed at you. Be genuine. The majority of criminal justice clients are street smart and intuitive. They will sense if you are being real. If you are not open and honest with them you will lose your credibility as being someone that can help them. It is appropriate if you are feeling anxious or unsure about a challenge directed at you that you let the group know.

However, it is especially important with this particular population of clients that the therapist does not indicate that they are uncertain about how to deal with the challenge posed against them.

Stage III - Initiative vs. Skepticism

During Stage III the therapist begins to reap the rewards as a consequence of the hard work they put into their group's development during the first two developmental stages. Issues continue to arise during Stage III; however, they are dealt with quickly and efficiently by both the group and the therapist. The feeling of being safe and the level of trust and cohesiveness is high and group members feel hopeful that they will recover.

Hope is important during Stage III especially for a population that initially felt hopeless. The criminal justice offenders initially believed they were destined to remain in their hopeless life situations as a result of their past records and lifestyles. The communication level within the group is high as members take responsibility to work on their treatment plan goals, resolve early life developmental interferences, identify their high risk factors to re-offending and assist each other in developing their relapse prevention plans. They interact freely and openly and are willing to take risks by confronting each other, utilizing self-disclosure, and receiving and providing feedback. Members within the group feel respected and supported by other members and the therapist. When conflicts arise within the group during this stage they are dealt with directly and efficiently by the members demonstrating the good conflict resolution skills that were modeled by the therapist during previous stages of the group's development. Members are observed working on their goals and recovery not only within the group, but also outside the group. Many voluntarily choose to participate in Alcoholics Anonymous, Narcotics Anonymous or Offenders Anonymous to help them continue to build a pro-social support system for themselves.

As previously discussed, group cohesiveness is high during this stage of development which is excellent given the nature of the group member's psychopathologies, and the expectation by most untrained professionals that such a population that is considered untreatable, defensive and resistant would prohibit the development of trust and cohesiveness. However, as far as the group has come, and even though the group is now a working group, the therapist still has work to do in order to maintain the high level of cohesiveness and trust. During this stage, the therapist should:

1. Continue to provide group structure and positive reinforcement of desired individual and group behaviors.
2. Continue to model appropriate professional and therapeutic behaviors.

3. Continue to encourage individuals and the group as a whole to take risks.
4. Continue to keep individuals focused on their treatment plans and goals.

Stage IV - Success vs. Failure

There are extensive articles in professional journals and other publications regarding when successful termination from treatment is appropriate. However, because of the population of clients we treat, and considering where they were referred from, there is only one criterion for successfully terminating the client. Termination from treatment for the criminal justice client only occurs when all the identified problems, goals and objectives have been successfully resolved and there is a marked improvement in the client's attitude, thoughts, feelings, beliefs and behaviors. That is unless the referring court has mandated otherwise or other criteria has been established. I personally terminate my client's group therapy when all the treatment plan requirements have been fulfilled as described above. This client is a success and a reflection of the success of the group from which they are being terminated. Professionally and ethically, I can't justify keeping a client beyond this point. Criminal justice clients aren't stupid and they know when they are being taken advantage of because of their vulnerable situation with the courts or probation department. If the client made it through all the stages of the group, has successfully fulfilled their treatment plan requirements and is held beyond this point, all the work done in group, and all the progress the client has made may easily become undone.

Many clients won't make it through group successfully for

one reason or another. The most common reason for clients not making it through group is self termination, failure to comply with agency and treatment requirements and rules, probation violation, re-offending while in treatment, inability to abstain from substances, or absconding.

There will always be a percentage of criminal justice clients that won't make it through group therapy successfully regardless of how effective the therapist is or how cohesive a group may be. For many of those clients, the bottom line is they just aren't ready to change and may never change.

However, during Stage IV of a new group's development there will be clients that will be ready for termination. You may notice that some of these clients may become anxious in anticipation of being terminated. After all, group was a safe place for them to come where they have learned new social skills, how to solve problems and resolve conflicts, how to interact with others, have changed their distorted thoughts, feelings and beliefs, and have been working toward living a pro-social lifestyle. This is a scary time for those clients and it is not unusual for the client to suddenly discover a new problem that must be solved or to pull back in group and not participate. Others may have anxieties and fears if they will make it or not or if they will be able to implement what they have learned without the support of the group. During this stage the therapist should:

1. Make certain there is no unfinished business to be completed.
2. Assist the client in dealing with their anxieties and fears about termination. It is important to allocate the time needed for the client to share their anxieties and fears about being terminated from group. The therapist

should ask the client the following:

a) How do you think this group has helped you to change?
b) What are the most important changes you have made?
c) What was the main turning point for you that helped you to make the decision to change your life?
d) What was it like for you to be part of this group?
e) How can the group and I assist you right now in feeling better about your leaving the group?

3. Assist the client in ways they can implement what they have learned in group to their daily life after termination. Various techniques can be used such as role playing, psychodrama or writing out a new life story of how they think life will be for them and sharing it with the group.
4. Have the group give the leaving member feedback. Be certain to instruct the group to be certain to share also how the terminating member has also assisted them in making changes.
5. Reinforce the positive changes that the terminating member has made by verbalizing your observations of changes in the client's attitude, thoughts, feelings, beliefs and behaviors.
6. Discuss aftercare with the client and their involvement in a support group.
7. Let the client know there is an open door if they need support after termination, or if they feel a need to return. This is really important. Many

> clients leave treatment and do well for weeks or months until they experience barriers placed before them preventing them from continued recovery. When this happens the client needs support to persist in their recovery. You can expect if you have an open door policy to return that approximately 10-13% of your terminated clients will become self referrals in order to continue their recovery and to avoid re-offending.

Once you start an open-ended group and work through the four developmental stages as outlined above, new members that enter the group will learn not only from you but also from the other members as to how they may participate, resolve conflicts, solve problems, confront other members, give and receive feedback, and how to rely on the group for support and encouragement in changing their lifestyles. An open-ended group may last for years with new members entering and other members leaving successfully. I once had an open-ended group of criminal justice clients that lasted for over 12 years with members coming and going.

The length of time it will take to work through the above four stages of development will vary depending upon the characteristics of the group members as well as the skills of the therapist leading the group. Providing experiences that create cohesiveness will move the group through the first two stages more quickly. In a well run group where group members are challenged to participate, the group develops trust and moves into the working stage more quickly.

The above described four-stage group developmental model can be reviewed as a graph as shown in Figure 1.

Figure 1

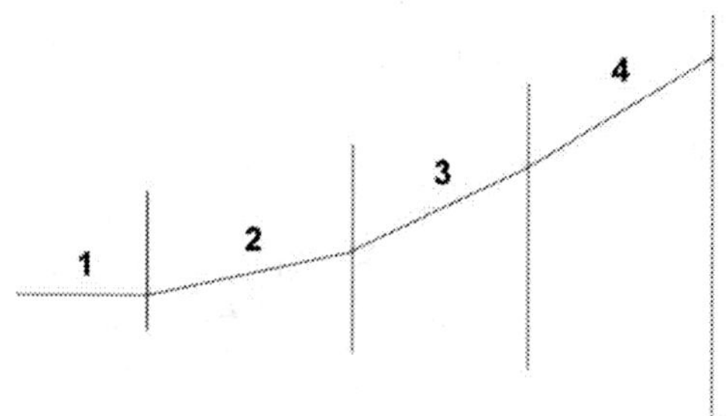

Termination Interview

The termination interview is helpful for several reasons including:

(a) Determining client satisfaction or dissatisfaction with the treatment they received;
(b) Assessing the effectiveness of group;
(c) Allowing the client to verbalize what they may need after termination that they may have been reluctant to share in the group;
(d) Using the results to make changes within the group structure or the group process that the therapist may not have realized;
(e) Enabling the client to see that their thoughts and observations are important helps them see that their treatment experience was beneficial.

Most criminal justice client programs don't take the time to do many of the functions that are required in agencies treating other types of clients such as developing a client criteria, screening clients for group, preparing clients for entering group, assessing the client's and the group's needs on an ongoing basis, and doing a client termination interview. This generally results in exactly what they set up for themselves: ineffective groups, high drop out and failure rates, high recidivism rates, dissatisfied clients, and a poor community reputation. The lack of providing professional and ethical services also contributes to the client's already poor self-image of themselves as being undesirable and untreatable which only serves to reinforce their antisocial lifestyle position.

Receiving feedback from the client as to their satisfaction or dissatisfaction with the services provided treats them as one would any consumer of mental healthcare services. Not to treat them as such discounts their significance and could result in an adverse outcome. Most states recognize that these practices do occur and have developed standards of care and services that court-mandated clients must receive; however, with the exception of substance abuse service agencies there is little or no monitoring as to their compliance.

The termination interview is a powerful tool that can be used to assess changes that may need to be made by the therapist or the group that could possibly assist in improving client retention in treatment. It also provides the client with the opportunity to discuss aftercare needs that they may have felt uncomfortable sharing in group, or didn't think of during the last time in group.

A very useful technique that I use when a client is being terminated from group is one that I learned from one of my trainers many years ago. It is called the Autonomy Termination Chair (Paschal, 1975). The autonomy chair is placed in the middle of the group and the group member being terminated sits in the chair. In this chair the group member asks the group, "Do you see me as fulfilling all my treatment goals and practicing a pro-social lifestyle?" The client restates their treatment plan goals, how they believe they behave, how they believe their attitude has changed, and what they believe they contributed to the group. The group and the therapist confront any contradictions between what the client being terminated states, and their observations, impressions, and concerns.

During this technique the therapist must make an objective assessment to establish whether the client leaving is real or if further treatment is indicated. The therapist must also be mindful of the possible recurrence of original symptoms, or even new symptoms that the client may suddenly become aware of or create. The therapist must also make due allowance for the affect of separation anxiety which is likely to be more acute in those group members who have identified more closely with the group member leaving, and with underlying fears that they will be abandoned. During this technique, the therapist should encourage the group to provide honest feedback to the client being terminated and to ask questions and make suggestions.

Using this technique to gain group feedback about their termination, the person leaving is maximizing personal, group and therapist resources. The group members know the member leaving in ways that no other people do. If the client is actually ready to be terminated from treatment and actually has made changes, then the autonomy chair serves to reinforce the changes the client has made. If they are not ready to be terminated and they are being "street slick" then their lack of readiness after group confrontation will be obvious.

The autonomy chair technique serves to bring together all the information the person leaving, the group, and the therapist possess about the individual leaving. It provides a means of objectifying termination anxieties for the group and the person leaving. It makes termination more therapeutic for everyone. It also provides the group with a procedure for resolving these problems and for further group intimacy (Paschal, 1975).

Determining the Success of Criminal Justice Intervention Programs and Groups

Does treating criminal offenders, sex offenders, batterers, and substance abusers really work? This question is asked at almost every training event or lecture I present on treating criminal justice clients. The answer is dependent upon how success is defined. Many times the definition of success is program self-serving and not very accurate. For example, if a substance abuser, sex offender, or batterer makes it through the treatment program without violating the group or agencies rules they are terminated and counted as a success. If the client relapses back into criminal acting out behaviors or use of drugs after termination it is seldom known because of the lack of client follow up, and not known until the client is referred back for further treatment after committing a new offense. Relapse is then not perceived by the program as being the program's fault. It is perceived as being the client's lack of motivation to continue their recovery. However, if the program did follow up with clients after termination in most cases relapse and possibly a new criminal offense could have been prevented.

Any program that points to evidence supporting the success of their program should be assessed with caution. However, offender programs that have lengthy follow-up procedures and don't just rely upon client's self report do have a lower rate of relapse.

Other factors that also contribute to a lower relapse rate include involvement in aftercare programs, self-help programs, and social support activities after the client is terminated.

Open Ended vs. Time-limited Groups

This chapter has been on open-ended groups that can continue for a length of time with no fixed time limit or end with clients entering and leaving the group at different times. I focused on open-ended groups because they are the most effective groups with criminal justice clients because of the eventual group culture that develops during the group's developmental stages. I did not spend any time on time-limited groups primarily because the group dynamics are different than those of the open-ended group.

Generally, in open-ended groups it is difficult, if not almost impossible, to work through any type of group development model because of frequent turn over of clients. This is not the case with criminal justice client groups because when the client is referred they are generally in treatment until the treatment plan goals have been fulfilled. Therefore, turn over is rather slow and the group population is somewhat stable for some time. If there is a frequent turnover at some point for one reason or another, but a significant number of older experienced group clients remain to pass down the group culture, the group will continue to evolve.

As I mentioned earlier in this chapter, my experience has been that criminal justice client groups have four identifiable developmental stages with issues that relate to the criminal justice client. The developmental stages also make it possible to work through them faster and more effectively than most other developmental models. The four stage model I am presenting in this chapter is characterized by the criminal justice client's initial concerns and issues in Stage I and eventually evolves into a group environment of support, trust, and cohesiveness in Stage IV. It should be noted that moving from stage to stage there will always be an overlap of issues from previous stages even when the group moves into the working stage of acceptance. I have attempted in the past to reduce the developmental stages to three, however, because of the heavy resistance, denial, conning and manipulating experienced working with this population, I found that three stages were an impossibility and not very practical.

Chapter 4: Best Practice Therapies

In the previous chapters, we discussed methods of selecting appropriate criminal justice client group candidates, preparing the client for group entry, group size, and how to develop a cohesive open-ended group by working systematically through the many issues that arise during the group's developmental stages. In this chapter we will focus on the particular models of therapy that may be used in groups that are considered best practice based upon empirical evidence rather than theory. In treating almost all types of criminal justice offenders, the use of cognitive-behavioral therapy is considered to be best practice.

It is almost impossible to review every cognitive-behavior therapy approach there is within this chapter. The term cognitive behavioral therapy is an umbrella term used to describe dozens of therapy theories. However, I did select several cognitive-behavioral therapies including Rational Emotive Behavioral Therapy, Reality Therapy, Moral Reconation Therapy, and Dialectical Behavioral Therapy based upon my clinical use of these procedures. Following is a brief description of these four therapies. The purpose of briefly discussing therapy models in this chapter is that it is important for a group therapist to have a theory of therapy they can utilize to facilitate client change.

Cognitive-Behavioral Group Therapy

Cognitive behavioral therapy (CBT) is comprised of two distinct theories that have been combined to create a more realistic therapeutic approach to modifying thoughts, feelings and behaviors. Under the above heading we will first focus on the cognitive aspects of CBT, and later the behavioral aspects of CBT.

CBT is a psychotherapy that is commonly used in treating criminal justice offenders to make changes in their distorted cognitions, feelings, beliefs, assumptions and behaviors with the intent to resolve their emotional difficulties that may have been interfering with their living a pro-social life. The particular CBT techniques that are utilized with criminal justice offenders in group therapy vary according to the client's needs, length and severity of their social problems, and type of crime they have been sentenced for, e.g., general criminal offending, domestic violence battering, substance abuse or sexual offending. However, most CBT groups treating criminal justice offenders commonly include keeping journals of their daily stressors that may be considered a significant high-risk factor to their re-offending and the thoughts, feelings and beliefs associated with the identified event or stressor. These journals are reviewed by the therapist who challenges and questions the distorted thoughts, feelings or beliefs that are generally contaminated by early life experiences and insufficient information in the attempt to change the client's frame of reference and try out new behaviors. For example, the following describes how the process works: Jason was abandoned by his father at the age of three. The loss and absence of his father resulted in extreme emotional pain. The experience and the resulting emotional pain led Jason to conclude that it was not safe to trust or to get to close to anyone because ultimately they would leave him. Now, at the age of 24, Jason was convicted of domestic violence battering. His wife states that Jason is a loner and she has been unable to get Jason to be open and close with her. Jason states that he isn't open and close to his wife because he believes that she will eventually leave him anyway. Jason's belief that everyone will leave him leads him to avoid true intimacy. He then confirms his negative belief to himself by battering his wife who then leaves him. This reinforces his belief that it is unsafe to trust or get close to others. In a CBT group, the efforts of the therapist would be directed at working to change Jason's distorted beliefs. This is accomplished by challenging Jason's thoughts, feelings and behaviors in response to trusting and getting close to others in an attempt to change his belief. If successful, and Jason changes his distorted beliefs, he may then become more active in his relationships with others, experience true intimacy, and reduce his own feelings of inadequacy.

CBT is not a brief therapy process and success does not occur over night. It many times takes months of hard work by the therapist and client to replace a contaminated cognitive-behavioral process with a more coherent process. The ultimate goal of CBT in offender groups is to identify the client's distorted thoughts, feelings, beliefs and behaviors that are related to their antisocial lifestyles and criminal acting out behaviors. It is also to ultimately discover how they are unreasonable, irrational, pathological and not conducive to the client living a pro-social lifestyle. (Aaron Beck, 1975) postulates "a person's core beliefs often formed in childhood contribute to "automatic thoughts" that arise in everyday life in response to situations." So you can well imagine that when you have a client such as Jason who formed his belief that it is not safe to trust or get close to others at age three, and you now have Jason at age 24, that success is not going to happen over night. In fact, it will be hard to change his beliefs because they have been reinforced for 21 years through Jason's negative behaviors in interpersonal relationships, resulting in people not wanting to be with him.

The cognitive aspect of CBT was developed by psychiatrist Aaron Beck during the 1960s. Beck came to the conclusion that the way in which people understand and ascribe a meaning to something was a key to therapy. The primary methods utilized in cognitive therapy is cognitive restructuring, assessing the validity of thoughts and beliefs, assessing attributions for the causes of events, and assessing what the client expects and predicts will happen – just like Jason did in our example.

The Behavioral Aspect of CBT

Part of treating criminal justice offenders in group therapy is the modification of behaviors that contribute to their personal and social problems. It is impossible to change a client's behavior unless the behavior is understood by the therapist. In order to fully understand a client's behavior a functional behavioral assessment of each behavior to be modified is needed. The simplest method of doing a functional behavioral assessment is the use of the ABC model.

The ABC model is where a careful observation of antecedents (what happened or what risk factor was present prior to the acting out behavior), behaviors (how the client responded to the event), and consequences (the relationship between the consequence, which is the payoff, and the cause). This procedure permits the group therapist to analyze and identify patterns of behaviors and also assists in identifying the client's offending cycle so that appropriate interventions can be designed to interrupt and modify the targeted behavior.

The scientific basis of behavior therapy is basically based upon the standards developed by Ivan Pavlov referred to as classical conditioning and operant conditioning developed by B.F. Skinner. In the following chapters, we will discuss some useful behavioral techniques that behavior therapy has contributed to and has been found to be successful in the treatment of general offenders, substance abusers, batterers and sex offenders and includes social skills training, habit reversal training, contingency management, systematic desensitization, assertiveness training, relaxation training, paradoxical intention techniques, and aversive therapy techniques.

Rational Emotive Behavior Therapy (REBT)

As you can see, CBT is a generic term for multiple types of therapies that share common characteristics. The very first form of CBT was developed by a New York psychologist, Albert Ellis, during the early 1950s and was referred to as Rational Emotive Therapy (RET). Ellis eventually changed

RET to Rational Emotive Behavioral Therapy (REBT). The concepts and contributions of Ellis during the 1950s and Beck during the 1960s were eventually combined and are referred to as cognitive-behavioral therapy or CBT. Today, the most common CBT method used to treat criminal justice offenders in group and individual therapy is Ellis's Rational Emotive Behavior Therapy (REBT) model because of its simplicity in its teaching, and the client's ability to apply its therapeutic concepts.

One of the underlying principles of REBT is that people who have a problem do not simply become upset by the problem, but rather through the way they create their view of reality based upon their beliefs about the problem. (Ellis, 2003) states "Humans, unlike just about all the other animals on earth, create fairly sophisticated languages which not only enable them to think about their feelings, and their actions, and the results they get from doing and not doing certain things, but they also are able to think about their thinking and even think about thinking about their thinking." Ellis also points out that "because of their self-consciousness and their ability to think about their thinking, they can very easily disturb themselves about their disturbances and can also disturb themselves about their ineffective attempts to overcome their emotional disturbances." Although this is the most basic part of REBT thinking, it is of great importance and directly relates to the problems of most criminal justice offenders.

In REBT group therapy, the group is taught the ABC model of disturbance and change. It is explained to the group as a whole that it is not just A (what occurs in the environment or activating event which can be external or internal) that creates a problem for them that leads to their negative emotional and behavioral consequences at C, but rather what their belief was about the activating event at B (their belief pertaining to A) which is their belief system. If the belief at B about A is a distorted belief, the consequence at C will more than likely be a negative one. If the group can understand this concept, they can learn to identify their beliefs about events and their high-risk factors that lead them to offend, and then begin to D which is to dispute and challenge their B beliefs and hopefully replace their beliefs about A which will result in avoiding a negative C consequence.

The CBT group therapist should be forceful and active in disputing their client's distorted thinking and belief system. The therapist should assist the group members to challenge their distorted beliefs (B). The disputing process combines cognitive, emotive and behavioral methods in order to attain the desired result of modifying the client's distorted (B) belief. The result of (D) disputing the client's distorted (B) belief about (A) and replacing it with a rational belief should result in the desired effect of a new philosophy (E). Through the use of cognitive, emotive and behavioral methods the client will learn effective new ways to deal with their problems and high-risk factors by disputing, challenging, and questioning their distorted thoughts and belief system which will result in healthier emotions and behaviors. One of the main goals of REBT is to prove clearly and convincingly to the group that when they encounter a high-risk factor, or experience an unpleasant event, they do have a choice of how they can feel and behave.

By becoming aware of their distorted thoughts, feelings, and beliefs, and their choices, they are more likely to lead a pro-social lifestyle. (Ellis, 2003) states that "People are born and reared with the ability to look at the data of their lives, particularly the negative things that happen to them and their goals and interests, and to make inaccurate inferences and attributions about these data." He also points to three core beliefs that he believes humans disturb themselves with, which include the following (Ellis, 2001):

1. "I absolutely must, under practically all conditions and at all times, perform well (or outstandingly well) and win the approval (or complete love) of significant others. If I fail in these important and sacred respects, that is awful and I am a bad, incompetent, unworthy person, who will always probably fail and deserves to suffer." For the criminal justice client dealing with early life abandonment issues for which they blame themselves this belief contributes to their feelings of worthlessness, being a failure, and depression most times resulting in their failure in relationships.
2. "Other people with who I relate or associate, absolutely must, practically under all conditions and at all times, treat me nicely, considerately and fairly. Otherwise, it is terrible and they are rotten, bad, unworthy people who will always treat me badly, and do not deserve a good life and should be severely punished for acting so abominably to me." This belief for many criminal justice clients that are gang members leads to anger, rage and revenge that may contribute to gang wars, killing, fights and other acts of violence.
3. "The conditions under which I live absolutely must at practically all times, be safe, favorable, hassle-

> free, and quickly and easily enjoyable, and if they are not that way it's awful and horrible and I can't bear it. I can't ever enjoy myself at all. My life is impossible and hardly worth living." Such a belief as this contributes to anxiety, depression, anger, and feelings of worthlessness and dissatisfaction for those criminal justice clients born and raised in dangerous environments such as slums, ghettos, barrio, or other poor environment that is unsafe and less than desirable. Such feelings and beliefs can lead to illegal activities in an attempt to have their piece of the "American dream."

A simplified example of the ABC model technique is as follows and diagramed in Figure 2 below:

A (the activating event): I'm broke, no job, no money, and there's a person alone over there that looks like they have some money on them.

B (the distorted or irrational belief): If a chump just stands there alone counting his money like that he deserves to be robbed, and I'm broke.

C (consequence of distorted belief at B): I feel anxious, scared and angry because I'm broke. I may get caught and go to jail.

D (dispute the distorted or irrational belief in B): Who or where does it say that people can't count their money in public and be safe. It isn't very smart, but they don't have to be robbed because of it. And so what if I have no job today, I may have one tomorrow and things will be better for me. I could also ask my family or a friend to loan me some money until I get on my feet. I don't have to worry about going to jail either.

E (new thinking to replace B): I would like to have money and a job, but right now I don't. So, just because I'm broke and don't have a job right now doesn't mean I have to harm someone by robbing them, and possibly go to jail. I don't need to feel anxious, scared or angry.

Figure 2

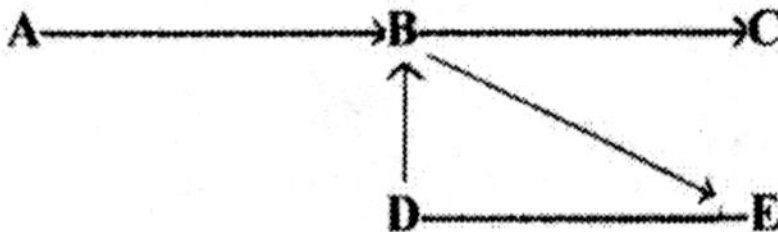

I always recommend that if the group therapist is going to use the ABC model with their groups that they teach it to the group clients during Stage I of the group's development because it then becomes an educational process that will also assist the clients to work through some of the developmental issues that arise during Stages II-IV. It becomes a powerful tool for the client to identify their irrational and self-defeating beliefs not only pertaining to their high-risk factors and other events in their lives, but also in the resistance, denial, anxieties, fears and conflicts they experience during the group's developmental stages and at time of termination.

It is also important for the therapist to understand that some therapies just don't fit well for some clients. In other words, even though REBT is extremely effective with the majority of criminal justice clients in group counseling some clients may require a somewhat different approach when identifying their risk factors and solving their problems. Therefore, it is advisable to have other tools available when these situations arise. It is similar to a craftsman having a bag of tools available in order to complete his work appropriately and professionally. In the mental health profession, we refer to possessing multiple therapeutic tools to solve a problem as the therapist being eclectic in choosing from a variety of techniques to solve the client's problem. Below, I will briefly discuss several other therapies that have been proven successful in treating criminal justice clients in a number of therapeutic settings.

Transactional Analysis

One of the most effective approaches to treating offenders, and one of my therapeutic tools, is Transactional Analysis. Transactional Analysis not only identifies the offender's distorted frame of reference but also offers a practical conceptual framework to identify and understand how offenders interact with others. It is for the most part believed that the offender's interactions with others contribute to their criminal acting out behaviors. It is also believed that a thorough understanding of the dynamics of the offender's interactions and their modification may prevent future criminal behaviors. A Transactional Analysis approach to offender treatment or counseling can be accurately described as being cognitive behavioral and affective because it effectively deals with the offender's distortions in all three spheres and their restructuring.

Transactional Analysis is a theory of personality developed by Eric Berne in 1961 and is in effect an all-inclusive heading under which there are four separate but relative areas as follows:

1. Structural Analysis, which is the analysis of the personality according to the Parent, Adult, and Child ego states.
2. Transactional Analysis is a theory of personality and social action. A clinical method of psychotherapy based on the analysis of all possible transactions between two or more people on the basis of specifically defined ego states.
3. Game Analysis which is the analysis of ulterior transactions which lead to the offender's negative payoffs.
4. Script Analysis which is the analysis of specific life dramas which the offender compulsively acts out.

In the following discussion, we will explore the concept, as well as the diagnosis, of ego states which may seem similar to Freud's theory of super ego, ego, and id. However, in Freud's theory of ego states the id and superego are not capable of being behaviorally observed, whereas the Parent, Adult, and Child can be understood and behaviorally observed and dealt with in Transactional Analysis treatment.

The Ego States

The diagnosis of ego states are behavioral, historical, and phenomenological which assists the therapist in determining which ego state the offender is in at any given time. Each of the ego states – Parent, Adult, and Child – have distinct and individual characteristics. Ego states manifest themselves clinically in two forms: either as coherent states of mind which is experienced as being "the real self," or as being intrusions into the real self. There are four directives to diagnose ego states which are:

1. Tone of voice
2. Demeanors
3. Gestures
4. Vocabulary

Parent Ego State: The Parent ego state contains all the things that were taught to the offender when they were young by their parents, substitute parents, and authoritative figures. Incorporated within the Parent ego state are all the rules, values, beliefs, morals, opinions and prejudices (internal frame of reference) that were learned that becomes an uncensored system of recordings with which the offender approaches every aspect of their life.

When the offender is in their Parent ego state they act out, think and feel the same as they perceive their parents did in similar situations and make decisions on the basis of this uncensored system of recordings which may or may not be appropriate for the here and now. In offender treatment it is generally the cognitive restructuring of the offender's parental frame of reference that will be required. The parent ego state can be both critical and nurturing and can be diagnosed by the following:

Critical Parent

Tone of voice: authoritative, critical, scolding, shaming, loud.
Demeanors: rigid, long suffering, respectable.
Gestures: pointed finger, hands on hips, head up high.
Vocabulary: do, don't, should, should not, never, every time, always, etc.

Nurturing Parent

Tone of voice: soothing, comforting, understanding, concerned, soft.
Demeanors: protective, comforting, soothing.
Gestures: hugging, healing, open arms.
Vocabulary: it will be alright, supportive words, offering alternatives, I love you, you're good, etc.

Adult ego state: The Adult ego state is adapted to current reality and in psychologically healthy persons is the executive of the personality and is not influenced by archaic parental rules, values, beliefs, morals, opinions or prejudices. It is that part of the person which is primarily engaged in objective data processing and computing probabilities. The Adult ego state is like a computer that uses facts to make a decision. The Adult ego state is diagnosed as follows:
Tone of voice: clear, precise, level, appropriate, well modulated.
Demeanors: alert, competent, relaxed.
Gestures: indicative, action oriented, instructive.

Vocabulary: what, when, where, how, probably, information seeking.

Child ego state: The Child ego state is that with which we were born with. While the Parent ego state is the recording of early developmental external events, the Child ego state is the recordings of the internal reactions (feelings) that occurred as a result of early developmental external events. The Child ego state should be free, intuitive, creative, and spontaneous and contains feelings, wants, and needs. When the offender is in their Child ego state they will act and feel the same way that they did when they were a child. If the offender's early life experiences were negative it is most likely that the Child ego state contains negative feelings and will not be free, intuitive, creative, or spontaneous, but is more manipulative, conning, lying, and slick in getting what they want and need. It is beyond the scope of this book to thoroughly describe in detail the various parts of the Child ego state which are the natural Child, the adapted Child, and the Little Professor.

The Child ego state is diagnosed as follows:

Tone of voice: (Natural Child) laughing, crying, giggling, rage, (Adapted Child) high pitched, whining, annoying, (Little Professor) whatever it take to get what it wants or needs.

Demeanors: (Natural Child) happy, scared, sad, free, adventuresome, (Adapted Child) innocent, naive, coy, guilt laden, (Little Professor) similar to the Adult but manipulative.

Gestures: (Natural Child) spontaneous and creative, (Adapted Child) squirming, pouting, hitting, withdrawing, showing off, (Little Professor) anything it takes to get what they want or need.

Vocabulary: (Natural Child) anything, (Adapted Child) lying, can I, may I, yes but, (Free Child) anything.

Psychopathologies

There are two types of psychopathologies in Transactional Analysis described as exclusion which is an observed rigidness in one ego state, and contamination which is the intrusion of the Parent or the Child ego state in the boundary of the Adult ego state. (Berne, 1961) described ego boundaries as being thought of as semi-permeable membranes through which psychic energy (cathexis) can freely flow from one ego state to another. This is observed when we see a person changing ego states in order for their behavior to be appropriate to a situation or occasion. Whenever there is an exclusion or contamination the free flow of psychic energy is disrupted.

Exclusion

Exclusion occurs when the offender reaches a decision that it is safer to operate from one ego state most of the time. Here the Adult ego state doesn't function well because some information is missing. This pathology can be diagrammed as shown below in Figure 3:

1. The Parent is excluding both the Adult and Child ego states.
2. The Adult is excluding the Parent and Child.
3. The Child is excluding the Parent and Adult.

Figure 3

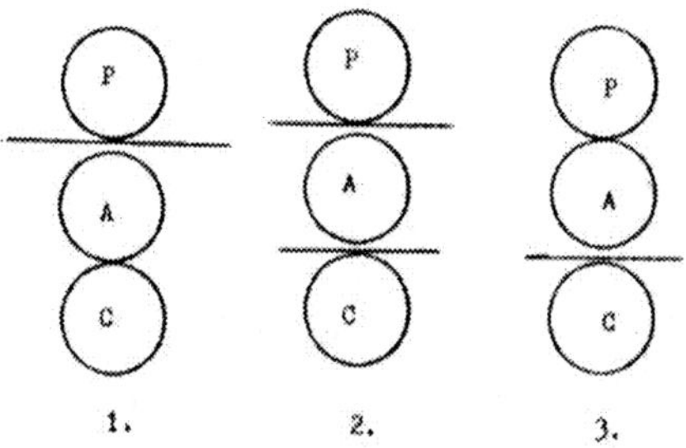

Contamination

The only ego state that can be contaminated is the Adult by either the Parent or the Child, or by both simultaneously. It is best illustrated as the Parent ego state rules, values, beliefs, morals, opinions and prejudices on the one hand, and the wants, needs, feelings and delusions of the Child ego state on the other. When this occurs the Adult ego state is using untested information to make decisions and the decisions that are made will be prejudiced or confused. The diagram in Figure 4 below shows the Adult contaminated by the Parent, the Adult being contaminated by the Child, and the Adult being contaminated by both the Parent and Child ego states.

Figure 4

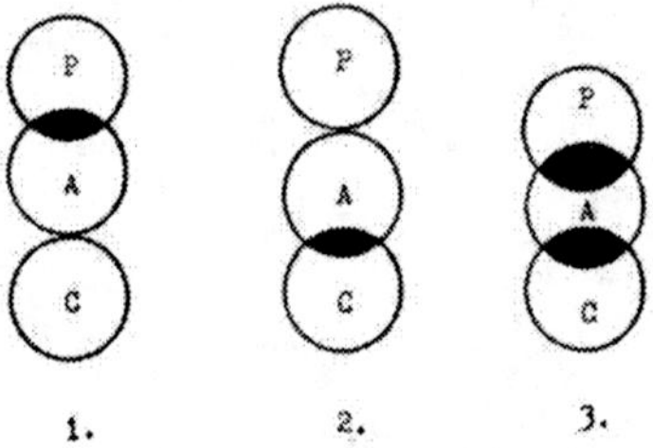

Transactional Analysis Proper

In Transactional Analysis there are four basic types of transactions that require a stimulus (S) and a response (R) which are complimentary. This means that when you address a certain ego state in a person the appropriate response is from the ego state addressed. When crossed it means that when you address a certain ego state in a person, the person responds from a different ego state. And, ulterior transaction which means the transaction has two levels of communication being the social level of what is being said, and the psychological or hidden message. For example, when a boy meets a girl he is attracted to he may say, “Hi, I noticed you are looking at that new movie advertisement. I’d love to see that movie myself.” That’s what was said on the social level, however, on the psychological level it may well mean, “I’d love to take you to that movie.” These transactions are diagrammed as below in Figure 5.

Figure 5

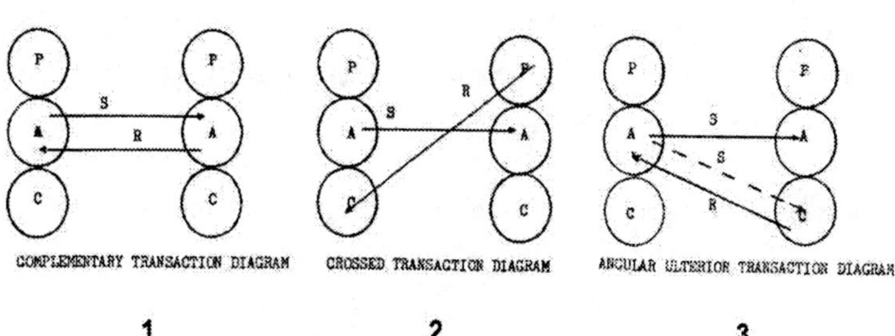

Reality Therapy (RT)

Reality therapy (RT) was developed in the early 1960s by psychiatrist Dr. William Glasser. During the 1970s, Glasser extended the RT concepts in what he referred to as Control Theory. The still-evolving concepts from RT to CT during the 1990s began to be described as Choice Theory which Dr. Glasser prefers today. However, the practice of RT is the basis of both theories. Reality therapy has a few things in common with REBT in that it moves the client away from dwelling on the past and focuses on the client's here and now self-defeating behaviors. It also shares with REBT in that it is a directive approach and is also didactic and action oriented. However, unlike REBT, it recognizes the problems that are inherent in labeling antisocial behaviors irrational and instead uses the term irresponsible. However, RT does not hesitate to point out any identified irrational thinking the offender may participate in, just as REBT does not hesitate to point out irresponsible behaviors.

Glasser believes that that those who engage in criminal activities suffer from the inability to fulfill their basic life needs adequately which include:

1. Survival: This includes our need for food, water, clothing, shelter, and personal safety.
2. Love or belonging: This includes being part of a group, family, or having a significant other.
3. Power: This includes being able to achieve something, feeling like a winner, feeling worthwhile, and being able to learn.
4. Freedom: This includes doing something at one's own pace, being autonomous, being independent.

5. Fun: This includes having the ability and opportunity to experience pleasure and enjoyment.

According to RT theory, if these basic needs are not met the offender will fail to perceive correctly the reality of the world and will act out irresponsibly and not recognize the consequences of their behavior. In other words, for the offender to act responsibly they must be encouraged to face reality, but in order to face reality they must be assisted in fulfilling their basic life needs. The basic physical and psychological needs of love and to be loved, as well as the need to feel worthwhile, according to Glasser are interrelated.

According to Glasser, the person who loves and is loved will generally feel they are worthwhile and be capable of giving love in return (Glasser, 1965). When the offender has these needs met they are more likely to develop a pro-social identity. If they don't have the needs met they may develop an antisocial identity which may result in irresponsible social behaviors.

Reality therapy (RT) refers to the causes of antisocial behaviors, but strongly stresses that the cause of antisocial behaviors is not an excuse for the behavior. RT and REBT are compatible in the sense that both take the approach that the offender is ultimately responsible for their own identity and behaviors. RT also asserts that there is a growth force within the offender that strives for a success identity which RT works to activate by encouraging the offender to discover and learn who they are, how they interact with others, and how they can be accepted by others.

A reality therapy therapist generally checks out with the client if they are getting their needs met with three basic questions:

1. What do you want?
2. What are you doing to get what you want?
3. Is it working for you?

Glasser itemizes seven steps that the RT therapist must take to cause a meaningful change in any client's behavior. I made several modifications in these steps to fit the criminal justice client more specifically, they are:

1. Be involved with the client, develop a close therapeutic alliance, be warm, open and honest at all times. Maintain professional decorum and act as a positive role model.
2. Understand your client's personal history, but do not stress or give importance to it. Review all the official records that are available, but be certain to separate the client from their present and historical behaviors.
3. Assist the client persuasively to evaluate their attitudes and behaviors and assist them in discovering how they themselves through their distorted thinking, feeling, believing and behaving have contributed to their antisocial identity and failures.
4. Explore with the client alternative thoughts and beliefs that will be more beneficial to them in developing a success identity.
5. After the client has made a decision regarding alternative thoughts, beliefs and behaviors, get a detailed commitment in writing on a plan of change.
6. Once the client has made the commitment in

writing, make it clear that excuses for not following through with the written plan will not be tolerated. Stress to the client that it is their responsibility to fulfill all the requirements within the plan. The therapist should closely monitor the plan for evidence of progress and confront even minor deviations from the plan.

7. The therapist should never be punitive with the client; however, the therapist should allow the client to suffer the natural consequences of their behavior which may include being terminated from treatment, referred back to probation or the court for non-compliance. Any attempt to protect the client from any natural consequence as a result of their behavior only reinforces their irresponsibility and denies the self-directedness of their behavior. Protecting the client from any natural consequences also makes a fool of the therapist resulting in the loss of credibility with the other members in the group.

Reality therapy is a valuable tool that can be used very effectively with the criminal justice client population in group therapy. However, I do suggest strongly that if you are thinking of using this model that you read more comprehensively about the theory and practice of RT. A list of suggested readings is available at the end of this text.

Moral Reconation Therapy (MRT)

Most cognitive behavioral therapies focus on the connection between cognition and behavior, and take the stance that dysfunctional behaviors can be changed by modifying one's distorted thinking and belief system. Of course, this approach as applied to criminal justice offenders suggests that offenders think, feel and believe differently than other people as a result of their development, life experiences and early life decisions.

However, Moral Reconation Therapy (MRT), also considered a cognitive behavioral therapy, takes a different approach and suggests that criminal justice offenders have gone through a series of stages of moral development that has resulted in a lower level of moral reasoning that has contributed to their making the wrong choices that contribute to their criminal behaviors. Most research examining moral development has been supportive of this assertion, finding that both juvenile and adult criminal offenders use lower levels of moral reasoning (Allen et al, 2001). The MRT approach makes an effort to enhance the moral reasoning of criminal offenders as a method of reducing recidivism (Miller, et al, 1996). The approach begins with the assumption that when a criminal justice client enters into treatment they do so with learned lower levels of moral development with strong resistance towards change, low self-esteem, inability to delay gratification, poor self-concept, low ego strength and are narcissistic. The MRT approach to increase moral reasoning is achieved by utilizing the following components (Little, et al, 1988):

1. Confrontation and assessment of behaviors, beliefs, attitudes, and defense mechanisms.
2. Assessment of current relationships.
3. Reinforcement of positive behavior and habits designed to raise awareness and moral

responsibility involved with the means and the ends.
4. Positive identity formation through exploration of the inner self and goals.
5. Enhancement of self-concept through ego enhancing activities and exercises.
6. The development of a higher stage or moral reasoning.

MRT takes various scenarios and asks questions about activities and if they would be right or wrong in certain situations. The group is also taught thinking errors:

1. Discounting, minimizing, and mislabeling: "I'm only doing what everyone else does."
2. Blaming others: "It was her fault for dressing that way," and "she seduced me."
3. Self centeredness: "Me, me, me, it's all about me, no one else counts."
4. Assuming the worst: "Why not, it's going to happen anyway," and "Who cares."

MRT was originally developed in the 1980s by Drs. Gregory Little and Kenneth D. Robinson to confront criminal thinking and behavior in a systematic manner with the ultimate goal of a reduction in criminal behaviors. MRT has 16 modules that contain prescribed tasks and homework assignments that clients must complete and then present in group. The counselor then uses objective criteria to evaluate whether the work being presented meets acceptable standards. Separate formats have been developed since 1986 that directly addresses specific types of offenders (see Little, 2000).

Dialectical Behavioral Therapy (DBT)

Following is a description of DBT, which is an excellent treatment modality for working with antisocial personality disorders and in particular sexual offenders. However, as you can see it does require a thorough understanding of its concepts, training and experience in order to become completely comfortable in its practice.

DBT differs somewhat from most cognitive-behavioral therapy approaches. It is a psychosocial treatment approach that was developed by Marsha M. Linehan specifically for clients with Borderline Personality Disorder (BPD). However, it has been used quite effectively with sex offenders as well.

DBT is mostly based in behaviorist theory along with some cognitive therapy components; however, unlike cognitive therapy it also includes core mindfulness practice as a critical part of therapy. Core mindfulness skills are awareness of one's thoughts, actions, motivations and behaviors and play a central role in DBT. Core mindfulness skills include developing the Wise Mind as the client learns and practices DBT skills which can change behaviors, emotions and thinking patterns associated with their sexual offending. When the client develops the skills to achieve Wise Mind they are in control and not trapped in all-or-nothing thinking and are better able to focus on what is effective and functional. In order to understand Wise Mind, one must understand two other states of mind referred to in DBT as Reasonable Mind which is when one is thinking logically and rationally, and Emotion Mind which makes logical and rational thinking difficult. A comprehensive reading on DBT that explains in detail, which is not possible in this book, is Cognitive Behavioral Treatment for Borderline Personality Disorder, by Marsha M. Linehan, ISBN: 0898621836.

There are basically two parts to DBT therapy which include:

1. An individual component. During individual component the therapist and the client discuss any issues such as risk factors or stressors that may arise during the week which are recorded within the client's journal or on diary cards which then follow a treatment target hierarchy such as:
   a) Encountering a high-risk situation and being tempted to offend.
   b) Therapy/treatment interfering behaviors such as lapses.
   c) Developing alternative coping behaviors.
   d) Working towards practicing new behaviors.

   During the individual session the therapist and client generally work on developing the necessary skills to practice the new behaviors, as well as any barriers that may exist which may interfere with the client applying the new behavior.
2. Skills group, which generally meets weekly for two-and-a-half hours, where the client learns to use their new skills which are broken down into four modules which include:
   a) Core mindfulness skills
   b) Emotion regulation skills
   c) Interpersonal effectiveness skills
   d) Distress tolerance skills

Interpersonal Effectiveness skills taught in DBT skills training is similar to other assertiveness, interpersonal problem solving, and conflict resolution classes. Sex offenders and most general offenders lack appropriate social skills. In their interactions with others they are generally lacking in skills of carrying out certain behavioral sequences such as asking someone out on a date, saying no, being appropriately assertive, resolving disagreements, etc.

Emotional regulation skills training with sex offenders are a critical component of sex offender therapy. Sex offenders are frequently emotionally intense and labile. Many are angry, frustrated, depressed and anxious when they are seen in therapy. Sex offenders can benefit by learning to regulate their emotions which when unregulated can lead to sexual offending. The DBT skills taught for emotional regulation (Holmes, et al, 2005) include:

a) Identifying and labeling emotions
b) Identifying obstacles to changing emotions
c) Reducing vulnerability to emotions
d) Increasing positive emotional events
e) Increasing mindfulness to current emotions
f) Taking an opposite action
g) Applying distress tolerance techniques

Distress Tolerance skills in most sex offender treatment programs generally focus on changing distressing events such as the sex offender's high-risk factors which most times cannot be done, or developing other alternatives. This is good, however, only a few programs that I am aware of teach the acceptance of the high-risk factor and learning to tolerate the distress associated with it. According to DBT theory, distress tolerance skills have to do with the ability of an individual to accept the current situation. In the case of a general offender or sex offender, it means coming into contact with a high-risk factor. Developing distress tolerance behaviors are concerned with tolerating, accepting, and surviving the stressor of the risk factor or crisis.

DBT utilizes four sets of crisis survival strategies that are also taught which include:

a) Distraction techniques
b) Self-soothing or calming techniques
c) Improving the moment
d) Thinking pros and cons

The DBT acceptance skills that are taught are:

a) Radical acceptance
b) Turning the mind toward acceptance
c) Willingness vs. willfulness

Develop a Motivational Counseling Style

Motivational Interviewing (Miller and Rollnick, 1991) was first developed specifically for the addictions field over a decade ago. Because of its effectiveness in motivating clients to change, it has expanded to the corrections, criminal justice system, and the forensic counseling fields as well. A Motivational Interviewing counseling style is a way of talking with the criminal justice client that is change focused and is not confrontational, argumentative, or threatening. It is an effective tool for dealing with resistance, difficult situations, a client's ambivalence to change, program violations, deception, and assists the client in preparing for change.

In the forensic counseling and substance field, the court-mandated client's motivation to make any changes in their use of substances or their antisocial lifestyles has been one of dissatisfaction. Historically, if a client was not motivated to be in treatment because of their criminal acting out behavior or substance abuse, and failed in treatment because of their lack of motivation it was considered to be the fault of the client. They lacked motivation. In fact, (Beckman, 1980) states that motivation has to be a requirement for treatment, without which the therapist would not be able to achieve much with the client.

Most clients that are mandated from the criminal justice system to attend treatment are cognizant of their substance abuse behaviors and antisocial lifestyles as well as the dangers they present. However, they disregard these dangers and continue to abuse substances and live their antisocial lifestyles anyway. When they first enter into a treatment or counseling program their intentions are usually good because they want to either stop using substances, or they want to stop living their present life style of crime.

However, at the same time they are unenthusiastic and cautious. The client being unenthusiastic and cautious is not a manifestation of denial or resistance, but is rather an intrapsychic conflict or ambivalence about change which is normal and can be resolved.

According to (Miller and Rollnick, 1991), the client's lack of motivation could be a manifestation of their ambivalence.

Adapting a motivational interviewing counseling style can assist in sorting out and resolving the client's motivational conflicts that could become a barrier to their progressing in treatment or counseling. Using a motivational style of counseling provides the opportunity to explore and resolve the client's conflicting attitude toward change.

Motivational interviewing increases the capability for beneficial change that everyone possesses (Rollnick and Miller, 1995). However, motivational interviewing and counseling do require study and training, because "Motivational Interviewing is a way of being with a client, not just a set of techniques for doing counseling (Miller and Rollnick, 1991)."

Motivational Interviewing is a counseling style based on the following assumptions:

1. Ambivalence about substance use and change is normal and constitutes an important motivational obstacle in recovery. (Author's note: this ambivalence towards change applies to general offenders and sex offenders as well.)
2. Ambivalence can be resolved by working with your client's inherent motivations and values.
3. The alliance between you and your client is a shared partnership to which you each bring important knowledge.
4. An empathetic, supportive, directive, counseling style provides circumstances under which change can occur. High confrontation tends to increase client defensiveness and in doing so reduces the probability of positive behavioral change.

In Motivational Interviewing there are five general principles that the therapist adheres to, they are:

1. Express empathy. The therapist's understanding of the client's experience assists in the client examining their ambivalence and facilitates change.
2. Avoid argumentation. Argumentation increases resistance and contributes to clients dropping out of treatment and relapse.
3. Support self-efficacy. Believing that change is possible is a factor in making a change. The client can be assisted with developing a belief that they can change.
4. Roll with resistance. In Motivational Interviewing the therapist does not resist the client's resistance, but instead rolls with it to further explore the client's views. In exploring the client's views and concerns, the therapist may invite the client to explore a new perspective, but does not impose new ways of thinking.
5. Develop discrepancy. The therapist invites the client to examine the discrepancies between their present behavior, lifestyle, and their future goals while gradually assisting the client in seeing how their current behavior and lifestyle may be holding them back from achieving their future goal.

Are There Risks of Using CBT?

There really are no risks involved utilizing a CBT approach. There is the possibility of an adverse treatment outcome if an untrained or unskilled therapist utilizes a therapy model without proper training. There is also the possibility that regardless of how well-trained, experienced and skillful the therapist is that some clients will not benefit.

This can be expected, especially with criminal justice clients, or with clients that are suffering from multiple co-occurring disorders.

As a general rule based upon my clinical experience with the criminal justice client population, the majority do identify and understand their distorted thinking, feeling, and frame of reference that has contributed to their present situation and losing lifestyle.

Many of these clients do change their distorted thinking patterns which in return results in a change in their core belief system and their behaviors. They develop the necessary skills to solve their problems and conflicts which improve their self-esteem and feelings of self-worth.

Chapter 5: Stages of Individual Change

In this chapter we will try to answer the questions: How do I know my client is changing? How do I know that my client has changed? How do I know my group is developing? But the truth of the matter is that we really don't know unless we observe a significant change in the client's or the group's behaviors. Even then it is difficult simply because of the predominant characteristics of the clients with which we work. Most are excellent cons, liars, cheats and manipulators, and many of them are not only streetwise or jail wise, but also treatment wise. Many of our clients have been in treatment so many times they almost know as many models of therapy as we do and even anticipate what our next intervention may be with some accuracy. However, even if we don't know for certain, we do have some tools that can help explain and maybe even predict a client's success or failure in making behavioral changes. It also assists the therapist in understanding why some clients in group may be more advanced and others not as advanced in making changes in their thoughts, feelings and behaviors.

One such tool is the Transtheoretical Model (TTM) which has been proven to be reliable with a variety of disorders including substance abuse, domestic violence battering, sexual offending, general offending, as well as in healthcare issues such as overeating, smoking cessation, and others. Based upon comprehensive research done over more than 15 years, the transtheoretical model indicates that clients move through a series of five stages referred to as precontemplation, contemplation, preparation, action and maintenance, which also incorporates relapse in the modification of or adoption of a new behavior, or ending an old habit or behavior. The research on quite a few types of problems and behaviors has also indicated that there are certain predictors of progression through the various stages of change (Prochaska and DiClemente, 1983), including decisional balance (Prochaska, 1994), self-efficacy, and the process of change (Prochaska and DiClemente, 1983). Making any change in the way people think, feel, believe, or behave is a tough task. Just like anything else in life that we want to accomplish, change requires working through a systematic process in order for lasting change to be achieved. The transtheoretical model of change can assist the therapist to understand where the client is presently at in the treatment process, as well as assist the client in recognizing where they are at in the change process as a means of encouragement and their striving towards recovery from their problems.

The TTM model is described as being a model of intentional change that focuses on the decision-making processes of the client. It is also described as a theoretical integrative model of behavior change (Prochaska and Velicer, 1997), because it builds upon other theories that work well together and have been incorporated into the model.

Basically, the model describes the ways people change a problematic behavior or acquire a new positive behavior in its place. The processes of change are ten cognitive and behavioral activities that make possible the desired change. The model also involves cognitions, emotions, and behavior which rely solely on self report by the client. Honest self reporting in the beginning of treatment with criminal justice offenders is frequently a problem that is encountered during the first stage of the model until the client's resistance and denial are dealt with effectively.

The five stages of change are the key organizing construct of the transtheoretical model, which construes change as being a cognitive-behavioral process which involves progressing through a distinct series of stages. The five stages of change are summarized below.

Stage 1: Precontemplation. In the criminal offender treatment field this is where the majority of our clients are when they are first referred. They have no intention of changing their behaviors, are in denial and highly resistant. They typically are not very trusting of others, don't like getting close, con, lie, cheat, manipulate, have interpersonal relationship problems, and are unconcerned about the consequences of their behaviors and antisocial lifestyles. During the precontemplation stage, the client is not expected to take any positive action in the foreseeable future which is generally measured as being within the next six months. This impasse for the criminal justice client is not because they are uninformed about the consequences of their behavior and lifestyle, but rather because they are unmotivated and resistant. These issues, as you may remember from the previous chapter on group development, are dealt with during Stage I -- Trust vs. Mistrust. During the early stages of both the group's development and treatment, an active therapist seeks to engage their clients in the treatment process focusing on immediate and primary concerns such as (1) creating an environment that enables clients to make changes, and (2) to acknowledge their need to change. During the precontemplation stage of change where the client is not currently considering any changes, some useful techniques to overcome their resistance and denial you may want to consider include:

1. Work with the client's resistance by acknowledging their lack of motivation and readiness.
2. Make it clear in group that the decision not to change and stay where they are in their life is theirs.
3. Be supportive of the client and encourage them to re-evaluate their current situation, life problems and behaviors.
4. Assist the client and the group in self-exploration of their problems without pressuring them to make immediate changes.
5. Clarify to the client and group the risks of not changing and personalize the risk to the individual client.
6. Assist the client in acknowledging the existence of their problem:
   a) Number of arrests.
   b) Number of incarcerations.
   c) Self-created barriers within the community.
   d) Divorces because of their behaviors.
   e) Lack of employment.
   f) Lack of social control.
7. Assist the client in acknowledging the severity of their problem:

   a) Personally, financially, loss of freedom, loss of family or relationships, educationally, vocationally, employment, emotionally, psychologically, etc.
   b) On family, significant other, friends and community.
8. Assist the client in understanding the solvability of their problem:
   a) How behavior change may change their life.
   b) What is available to assist them in making changes.
   c) Provide the client with some examples of how they may solve their life problems.
9. Assist the client in identifying their ability to change their behaviors:
   a) Assist them in identifying their potential in doing or becoming something as a result of their changing.
   b) Their intellectual ability to change.
   c) Their physical health.

   Some useful interventions you may want to consider during this stage that may assist the client in moving into the next stage include:
   a) "What would have to happen in order for you to realize that X is a problem for you?"
   b) "What have been some indications for you that this may be a problem?"
   c) "What is the worst thing that could happen if you changed X?"
   d) "What is the best thing that could happen if you changed X?"
   e) "How will you know it's time to change?"

Stage 2. Contemplation. During the contemplation stage

the client is intending to change in the near future. According to the TTM model, this means within the next six months. During this stage, clients become aware of the pros of changing their behaviors and lifestyle; however, they are still aware of the cons in changing which are usually:

a) What will I do instead?
b) How do I do this?
c) How will I make new friends?
d) What will others think of me?
e) Is it really going to be better for me if I change?

Choosing between changing and not changing for most criminal justice offenders that have become firmly entrenched in their lifestyles over many years can produce profound confusion and uncertainty.

These issues are dealt with during Stage II of the group's development: Acceptance vs. Rejection. The client is experiencing high levels of anxiety about committing to change that has to be confronted and dealt with openly in the group. The TTM model generally labels clients that become stuck in Stage 2 as being not ready for traditional action-oriented programs. However, we are not able to label our clients as such because we expect behaviors like resistance, denial, and procrastination, and fully understand the pathological nature of our client's problems and that they can be worked through successfully resulting in acceptance to change. It is important during this stage of change that the therapist acknowledges the feelings that their client and the group as a whole is experiencing. Most criminal justice clients have difficulties getting in touch with and communicating their feelings during the earlier stages of treatment. The therapist, during this stage of group development and individual change, should assist the client in labeling their feelings. This is the first step in emotional management and the ability to empathize with the feelings of others. If a client appears to be stuck in Stage 2 of change it is useful to:

1. Continue to work with the client's resistance by validating their ambivalence about changing their behavior and what they are feeling when contemplating change.
2. Continue to clarify and reinforce the probability that nothing will change for them, and the decision to not change is theirs.
3. Assist the client and the group as a whole to evaluate the pros and cons of changing their behavior and lifestyles. You can make the evaluation process a group exercise which will possibly assist other members in accepting change. To complete the process, have each group member write out their personal pros and cons and then have each group member share it with other group members during the group session. The client's weighting of the pro and cons of change are the decisional balance construct of TTM. It is derived from the Janis and Mann's model of decision making (Janis and Mann, 1985) which includes four categories of pros which are instrumental gains for self and others, and approval for self and others. The four categories of cons are instrumental costs to self and others, and disapproval from self and others.
4. Assist the individual member and the group to

identify and promote a new positive life position and outcome projections for their future. Some useful interventions during this stage that can assist in moving the client to the next change stage are:

a) "What can the group do to help you at this time?"
b) "What would help you at this time?"
c) "What has happened to make you consider changing?"
d) "What do you think will prevent you from changing?"
e) "How do you think it would be better for you if you change?"
f) "What do you think you need to learn about changing?"
g) "What have you tried in the past?"

Stage 3. Preparation. This is the working stage for both the group and the individual client that has decided that change may be needed. The client intends to take action in the immediate future, which according to the TTM model of change is measured as the next month. The individual client, as well as other group members, are planning and committing to doing something, such as attending Alcoholic Anonymous, Narcotic Anonymous, Offenders Anonymous support group meetings, or fulfilling a treatment plan goal. The preparation stage of individual change corresponds with the group's developmental Stage III which is Initiative vs. Skepticism. During the preparation stage the client is still somewhat skeptical about making changes in their life; however, they are taking the initiative to do something. During this critical stage of change the therapist should:

1. Assist the client in identifying any barriers to their intended change.
2. Reinforce the importance and need for social support.
3. Provide reinforcement for the desired change.
4. Encourage the client to stay focused on their behavior change goal.
5. Identify if the client has the skills to achieve the change.
6. Support the client and group as a whole to take risks to change.
7. Encourage the client to take small initial steps in making the change.
8. Reinforce the client's abilities to change if they desire to.

Stage 4. Action. This is the stage in which clients have made obvious changes in their behaviors and lifestyles that they have been practicing for the past three to six months. In the TTM model not all modifications of behavior are counted as action. During this stage, only complete abstinence from their antisocial lifestyles or whatever other problem they are being treated for, such as alcohol or drugs, counts as action. This stage of action corresponds to the group's developmental Stage IV- Success vs. Failure. Most criminal justice offenders during this stage of change continue to make the difficult decisions needed during the action stage of treatment and change; however, they may still be prone to relapse depending upon the length and severity of their problem. In any event, the client's new thoughts, feelings, beliefs and behaviors continue to result in the development of a pro-social lifestyle. During this stage of personal change for the client, the therapist should focus on:

1. Continuing to develop coping behaviors for high-risk factors.
2. Reinforcing the client's pro-social behaviors.
3. Assisting in working through feelings of loss that most clients experience when changing their lifestyles or abstaining from alcohol or drugs, by reinforcing both the short-term and long-term benefits of their change.
4. Reviewing with the client the effectiveness of their relapse prevention plan.

Stage 5. Maintenance. This is the stage where the client works on their relapse prevention plan to prevent relapse. During this stage, the client is stronger in their recovery than they were in the action stage. They have been practicing their new behaviors, reaping the rewards of their new pro-social lifestyle and are less tempted to relapse as they become increasingly confident that they can be successful. The self-efficacy construct of TTM signifies the confidence that the client has that they can cope with their high-risk situations without relapsing to their unhealthy or high-risk behaviors. If the client does relapse at some point during their maintenance stage very few regress all the way back to the precontemplation stage. My experience, as well as others that use TTM, has been that if the client should at some point relapse they generally regress back to the contemplating or preparation stage. Relapse is common during lifestyle changes.

The therapist can assist the client by explaining that if they do relapse, they have learned something new about themselves and the process of changing behavior.

By placing a focus on the positive part of the client's plan such as, "You haven't frequented a strip club where your drug dealer hangs out for three months. How did that work for you?" shifts the focus from "I'm a failure," to problem solving and provides encouragement for further recovery. This provides the client with support and re-engages their efforts in the change process. This type of intervention does not leave the client with a sense of "being a loser," and their efforts to continue in the change process should be acknowledged.

How Change Occurs

Regardless of the theory of change you may choose to use in your practice it is important to keep in mind that change is hard for anyone, and is especially hard for most criminal justice offenders because of their early life experiences and the lifestyle decisions they made based on those experiences. Making lifestyle changes by the criminal justice client requires that they make re-decisions based on new experiences that may occur in therapy. However, a re-decision by the client is not a promise to change. It is an intention to change which they may follow through with, and at times revert back to their old negative patterns. This may be a pattern that you will recognize with some clients as they work their way through the stages of change. This doesn't mean failure by the client or therapist. It means the client intended to make a change very much like a small child learns to walk; it will probably occur haltingly at first until it feels normal or OK to the client.

The motivation for most criminal justice clients to want to change has four sources:

1. Dissatisfaction with their present life situation.
2. Desire to live a different life and to think and feel differently.
3. Need for positive recognition from others.
4. Avoidance of any further negative consequences.

These four motivational factors are extremely important in moving the client into the different stages of change. Positive recognition from the therapist and the group for any different thoughts, beliefs or behaviors that are made is also a powerful motivator that can move the client into the next stage of change.

The process of change involves both covert and overt activities that the client utilizes in order to progress through the various stages of change. The process of making changes provides the therapist with valuable information for changing and designing interventions in each stage for the client. The ten processes (Prochaska and DiClemente, 1985) are independent variables that the client must utilize in order to move through each stage to the next. For clients to move from one stage to another they need to become aware that the advantages (the pros) of changing their behavior and lifestyle far outweigh the disadvantages (the cons). This is referred to in TTM as the decisional balance. They must also develop the confidence that they will be able to maintain the changes they make when they encounter their high-risk situations that may entice them back to their old behaviors and lifestyle. This is referred to as self-efficacy in TTM. The first five are experiential processes and are generally used in the early stages. The last five are behavioral processes that are used in the later stages of change. The following is a list of processes with a sample item for each process for the criminal justice offending client as alternative labels.

The Experiential Processes of Change

1. Consciousness raising (increasing the client's awareness of criminal behaviors): "This is my third arrest for the same thing."
2. Interventions that are carefully thought out and designed to increase the criminal justice offender's awareness of the causes and severity of their problems, as well as the consequences of their behavior on themselves, family, victims and community, not only increases their awareness, but also results in the client providing feedback which offers the opportunity for the therapist to identify and confront their distorted thoughts and beliefs.
3. Dramatic relief (emotional management and gaining social control): "I become excited and angry whenever someone confronts me. I really get scared when this happens. I think I can change this; others in group have."
4. During this process the client may experience high levels of anxiety or fear because of their behavior. They may even experience hope and encouragement when they see others in the group make changes. It is even possible that they may experience both feelings.
5. Environmental re-evaluation (social assessment of their behavior): "My behavior is harmful to myself, family and other people." The client becomes increasingly aware of how their antisocial lifestyle behavior has been harmful to self, family, and others.
6. Social liberation (new social opportunities): "The way I

approach others now doesn't provoke confrontations."

7. During this process the client realizes that the community is more supportive of their new behaviors and lifestyle.
8. Self liberation (taking a self inventory of their thoughts, feelings, beliefs and behaviors firmly believing they have the ability to change them): "My distorted thoughts and beliefs make me feel bad about myself. I can change them. I changed other things about myself, it will be hard, but I can do it."

The client during this process comes to believe in their ability to change and makes a commitment to act on their belief.

The Behavioral Processes of Change

1. Stimulus control (developing coping skills to deal with high risk factors): "I will avoid going to bars and strip clubs where I know drugs are available."
   The client uses reminders and cues that assist them in maintaining their new behavior and lifestyle.
2. Helping relationship (developing a social support group): "I can always talk to my counselor or AA sponsor if I get the tugs to re-offend."
   The client continues to develop a pro-social support system.
3. Counter conditioning (replacing what is being changed): "I really enjoy reading; it takes my mind off my old friends and lifestyle."
   The client finds healthy ways of structuring their

time replacing old unhealthy ways.

4. Reinforcement management (positive reinforcement for following their plan): "I will reward myself each time I get a tug to re-offend and I don't."
   The client finds ways to reward themselves for new behaviors such as going to a show, buying a new shirt, taking a trip, etc.
5. Self evaluation (continues to a moral and behavioral inventory): "I am firm in my commitment to never again commit a criminal act."
   The client continues taking a moral and behavioral inventory of themselves and continues making life changes. The client commits to a pro-social life as their new life style becomes ego syntonic: "this is who I am."

The transtheoretical model is utilized more in programs for smoking cessation, addictions and other unhealthy behaviors. TTM has not, to my knowledge, been commonly utilized in the treatment of criminal justice offenders. That is unfortunate because TTM can and does result in higher retention rates for those offenders attending longer term treatment such as in the case for sex offenders who are generally in long-term programs.

Traditional criminal justice offender programs have very high dropout rates because most programs do not fit the client's "here and now" treatment needs. Since the program or therapeutic approach does not meet their needs, they soon dropout. However, TTM is specifically designed to tailor interventions that are matched to the client's specific needs depending upon what stage they may be in. Since every intervention is tailor made to the client's specific needs at the time, clients drop out of treatment less frequently because of unreasonable therapeutic demands.

The TTM model of individual change will also give you some insight as to why some clients appear to be more advanced than others during treatment although they are all in the same group, and why the issues that are addressed during a group's developmental stages may also seem to overlap with each other. In each stage of the group's development, individual clients may be in different stages of individual change which is why issues overlap from one group development stage to another. This important insight into the process of change allows you to select or develop appropriate interventions not only for the group as whole, but also to assist the client that is stuck to move along the stages of change. Using this framework, the therapist identifies the stage of change and engages the client or group in a process to move to the next stage.

Chapter 6: Group Treatment Issues & Strategies

Although there are many similarities between male and female criminal justice offenders convicted of crimes and their common treatment needs, there are also dissimilarities in their personal treatment needs. In this chapter we will discuss the common and personal treatment needs of both genders. We will discuss male treatment issues first because the majority of offenders referred by the criminal justice system for treatment are men. Many of the issues that have traditionally been attributed to only women and thought of as being only women's issues have also been found to also apply to many male offenders as well. We will discuss these issues.

Male and Female Group Therapy Issues

The majority of offenders referred for treatment tend to share many common treatment issues that should be addressed within the group setting. However, they also tend to share characteristics that affect the treatment process. Common characteristics shared by most offenders are a long history of psychosocial problems and difficulties that have been empirically connected to their criminal lifestyles and substance abuse which include:

- poor interpersonal relationships that include difficulties with family members
- difficulty in maintaining a meaningful long-term relationship
- poor anger and conflict resolution skills
- poor stress management skills
- psychological problems and emotional disorders
- seeking and maintaining gainful employment
- lack of education and vocational skills
- social isolation
- poor social control
- poor living environment
- distorted cognitions and beliefs

These chronic psychosocial problems many times result in their suffering from poor self-esteem, high levels of anxiety, further social isolation, physical and or emotional deprivation, unsuccessful attempts at changing their antisocial lifestyles, homelessness, incarceration, and substance abuse. Although these psychosocial problems apply to a large majority of the criminal justice offender population they may not apply to all offenders. Therefore it is essential for the group therapist to assess and take into account the unique situation and needs of each individual client in their group. This statement may sound very basic, but the reality of most offender and substance abuse groups is that individual needs are not met.

Many times the individual needs are net met because the thinking is that all offenders and substance abusers are in the same situation and have identical problems and needs. This thinking has contributed to unfortunate adverse treatment outcomes for some of the clients referred to those programs by the courts.

You may be somewhat surprised that I included poor parenting skills in the above common characteristics for male criminal justice offenders. Male offenders may not discuss issues regarding their children unless they are asked. This happens because most offenders have difficulty admitting to their failure as a father. Being a good father is as important to the offender as it is to the non-offender. The primary difference is that most offenders feel inadequate because they have no idea what they should be doing as a father or how well they are doing it. Others feel ashamed because they don't have the financial resources to support a child because of their lack of vocational skills and the difficulty they have maintaining employment. Many offenders come from single parent families where the father disappeared from their lives early in their development, or they had a father that was incarcerated, an alcoholic or abusing substances who was a poor role model. Parent training can result in the offender taking financial responsibility for their child, to actively participate in their children's lives, be more accepting of their children, assist in developing a positive relationship with the child, motivate the offender to participate in their treatment program, and to seek a pro-social lifestyle.

It is also essential to address in group the criminal justice client's present offense, past offenses, and other criminal behaviors. (Antonowicz and Ross, !994) state the need to prioritize treatment according to the criminogenic needs of criminal justice clients, particularly the individual factors that led the client into contact with the criminal justice system. Generally, these factors are distorted thinking patterns, beliefs, values, and a lower level of moral reasoning or substance abuse. There are generally a wide array of problems associated with criminal behavior or substance abuse as a result of the offender's distorted thoughts, beliefs, values and lower level of moral reasoning that brings them to the attention of the criminal justice system including:

- their psychosocial problems
- their lack of social control
- their lack of impulse control
- their poor emotional management skills
- their poor problem solving and conflict resolution skills
- their lack of empathy
- their poor social skills

The identification of these common factors provides us with the information that is needed in order to develop the clinical strategies necessary to address the client's treatment needs. Below is a summary of the clinical issues that may be identified and will need to be addressed and modified during the course of treatment:

1. Improvement in interpersonal relationships.
2. Development of anger management skills.
3. Development of problem solving skills.
4. Development of conflict resolution skills.
5. Development of stress management skills.

6. Developing a support system.
7. Gaining and maintaining social control.
8. Developing impulse control skills.
9. Learning empathy skills.
10. Developing parenting skills.
11. Educational and vocational training.
12. Improving poor living environment, e.g., living arrangements, neighborhood, etc.
13. Dealing with distorted cognitions, beliefs and affective style.

Group Treatment Issues and Process

Group treatment should include all of the client's identified problems with a focus on their maladaptive and anti-social lifestyles. Most criminal justice clients identify with some or all of the above clinical issues as the major cause of their life problems. In the very beginning of the treatment process most offenders will minimize, rationalize or deny their problems. This rationalization or denial should be confronted by the therapist in a non-threatening, helpful manner utilizing motivational interviewing techniques. The therapist should identify and confront cognitive distortions that the client may engage in when discussing their life problems and antisocial lifestyle. The therapist should assist the client in learning alternative ways of dealing with problems by teaching them new skills such as cognitive restructuring for dealing with their problems.

Group treatment should also focus on victim awareness and the development of empathy. Empathy development is critical for both general offenders and sex offenders so the client can become aware of the impact their anti-social behaviors have on others and begin to take responsibility for their own behaviors. Many offenders have a history of domestic violence battering or other assault behavior because they lack the skills to effectively deal with anger-provoking stimuli. Teaching the client anger management and conflict resolution skills will assist them in dealing with their anger in socially acceptable ways.

When teaching the group any type of social skill, it is not very useful to ask them: "What did you learn tonight?" This opens the door for the group to basically repeat what they heard or what they observed. It is more useful to have each group member describe "how" what they have learned will assist them in living a pro-social lifestyle, and to discuss how they will transfer what they have learned in group to situations that occur outside the group. This creates an internal thinking process that not only assists in the further development of group participation and cohesiveness, but also lays the foundation for further learning. In the sections below, we will discuss cognitive distortions, cognitive restructuring strategies, and social skills development.

Cognitive Distortions

This section applies to both males and females. Contributing to the criminal justice offender's life problems are their distorted thinking patterns, beliefs, and low moral reasoning which will require considerable attention and restructuring during the course of treatment. My personal observations treating offenders has been that the development of their distorted beliefs and cognitions are generally a result of negative early life events occurring between the ages of 3-12 years prior to the full development of the prefrontal cortex. Their interpretation of an event results in a feeling which then results in a belief, along with corresponding rules, in order to maintain the belief in order to avoid negative and hurtful feelings in the future.

To make this process more clear, consider the following example:

(Event): James was abandoned by his father at age six.

(Interpretation): Daddy left home because I am a bad boy. He doesn't love me.

(Feeling): This really hurts, I feel sad and scared.

(Belief): Nobody loves me. If I love them they will only leave me.

(Rule): Don't get close to others and don't trust others.

The process from beginning to end is linear and can be diagrammed as shown in Figure 6 below.

Figure 6

Event------→Interpretation-----→Feeling------→Belief------→Rule

In order to successfully challenge a client's distorted belief about an event or person we also need to identify and understand the rules which allow the continuation of such a belief. The rules that sustain the distorted belief must also be restructured. If the rules associated with the belief are not changed then the challenging of the belief only results in a temporary interruption or change. Just as in sports, if the rules are in play the game continues on; if the rules are disrupted, the game stops temporarily. In other words, the temporary interference of challenging the belief without identifying and challenging the rules that sustain the belief only result in the eventual re-emergence of the distorted belief. My clinical experience has been that once the rule sustaining a distorted belief has been identified it can be connected to many of the other psychosocial problems that need to be addressed in treatment. Those problems were discussed above.

For instance, let's consider the above example with James being abandoned at age six. The abandonment resulted in his belief that nobody loves him, if he loves someone they will leave, and the rules sustaining that belief of "don't trust" and don't be close. Eighty-five percent of juvenile and adult offenders are from one-parent families where parental abandonment either physically or by the parent(s) not being emotionally or psychologically available has occurred. Such a belief and sustaining rules result in attachment issues and ultimately in a lack of affiliative orientation. This sense of not belonging and detaching from the human herd severely inhibits their ability to empathize with others that are not in the same life situation as they are. It also results in the repression of their feelings which involves a process of converting energy that is used to feel into acting out behaviorally. The repression of their feelings also contributes to the elimination of genuine affect from their personalities that result in them being thought of by others as being out of touch with their feelings and being emotionally immature, self-centered, not caring, and un-trustful. These thoughts further contribute to their sense of isolation which is utilized to separate their distorted beliefs from any genuine emotional component. For example, James may discuss in group therapy his father leaving his life in a very detached manner with little or no audible display of emotions:

"You're right, my father did abandon my mother and me -- it's no big deal. I guess you can say that I don't like him very much, oh well."

The rules that any individual creates to sustain a belief can vary. Rules generally contain a "don't, should or must" which are the governing principles that guide the client's actions or behaviors and allows the distorted belief to continue to exist. The most common rules that criminal justice offenders have a tendency to share for their various distorted beliefs are:

Distorted Rules

1. Don't trust
2. Don't be close
3. Don't feel
4. Don't think
5. Don't grow up
6. Don't exist
7. Don't belong
8. Don't succeed
9. Don't love
10. Don't be important

11. Don't be good
12. Don't be honest
13. Don't be happy
14. Don't try
15. Don't be smart
16. Don't listen
17. Don't have needs
18. Don't change
19. Don't be sane
20. Don't snitch

Distorted Beliefs

1. The system is crooked.
2. Most people are dishonest.
3. I deserve the very best.
4. The only way I can get what I need is to take it.
5. Nobody cares about me.
6. Women (or men) are only good for one thing.
7. Women/men are weak.
8. If I show that I care, others will think I'm weak.
9. To be respected, you have to be wealthy.
10. I have to be tough to survive.
11. Education isn't important.
11. People are fools.
12. Children enjoy sex as much as adults do (pedophiles).
13. If the going gets too tough, I'll kill myself.

The above only represents a very small sample of what the client's rules and beliefs may be. There are variations and, of course, many other rules and beliefs may contribute to their psychosocial problems. Many clients may have as few as one and others could have multiple distorted beliefs and rules that will need to be challenged and restructured.

The beliefs and rules the criminal justice client develops as a result of their interpretations could also be the result of early life attributions from a parent, relative or a significant person in their life.

An attribution defines or labels an individual as to what or who they are, and has the potential to contribute to the child's life course or script. For example:

(Event): "James you're bad. You're just like your father!"

(Interpretation): "I'm just like dad. I'm untrustworthy and evil inside. I'll probably die at 28, just like he did from drinking too much."

(Feeling): Scared and sad.

(Belief): No matter what I do I'll never be different from my father.

(Rule(s)): Don't try, don't succeed, don't be good, don't exist.

Once the belief(s) and rule(s) have been developed, the rule(s) become a self-fulfilling prophecy that unconsciously sets up situations for the individuals that reinforces their original interpretation and belief(s). For example, a client that has a belief that "all women take advantage of men and eventually leave" with corresponding rules of "don't trust and don't love" to avoid being taken advantage of may become assaultive in a relationship with a woman who asserts herself. He may take her actions of redefining her assertiveness to mean that she is disrespectful and is taking advantage of him as a man. Redefining refers to the mechanism that criminal justice offenders use to defend themselves against stimuli that are inconsistent with their beliefs and to maintain an established view of themselves, other people, and the world (their frame of reference) in order to further their life program or script. Redefining has three major components – denial, grandiosity and cognitive distortions – that should be challenged. This frame of reference becomes the client's mental pattern of thinking or cognitive schemas from which cognitive distortions are derived. The client's rules are the schemas that govern how they will interpret and react to any type of stimulus. In treating the criminal justice offender or an ASPD, their rules form the basic data of treatment.

In offender therapy, rather than focusing on insight resolving fears, wishes, or desires, the focus should be on identifying their rules and making them the focus of the therapeutic work. The therapeutic task could be conceptualized as one of challenging the client to develop an alternative rule which is the foundation of their distorted cognition(s) and belief(s). Again, just as in sports, there are rules to play the game correctly. If the rules change then how the game is played changes and that changes the entire game because the rules oversee and establish how the game must be played. The same concept applies here to changing the client's cognitive rules. There are then new rules, new cognitions, new beliefs and new behaviors. The work involved in identifying and assisting the client in making these changes is lengthy and requires considerable firmness and skills on part of the therapist. The therapeutic relationship should serve as a structure for examining the client's rules and beliefs. The identification of beliefs and rules should form a large part of the initial work in therapy. Once they are identified, they can be worked through in a variety of ways. One way is to challenge the cognitive distortion of the interpretation of the stimulus or event that lead to the cognitive belief(s) and rule(s) resulting in their present symptomatology.

Strategies for Changing Distorted Cognitions

If you begin challenging a group member's distorted cognitions too early in the group's development you will most likely have little or no success in getting through to them. As I work through the group's early developmental issues and identifying their cognitive distortions, I teach the group the REBT method that I will be using in their treatment, however, I don't challenge them. In the early stages of the group's development the level of denial and resistance is high and group cohesiveness is low. As the group progresses and moves into its working stage where there is a higher level of cohesiveness I begin utilizing various cognitive restructuring techniques.

Once a distorted rule or belief is identified the therapist generally asks a lot of questions focusing on the interpretation of the event or stimulus. A technique I generally use once the distorted belief and rule are identified is role play and role reversal in order to get the client in touch with their erroneous interpretations of the event or stimulus that resulted in their belief(s) and rule(s). Their interpretation is usually a result of the client making conclusions beyond the actual meaning of the event or stimulus. Once the client becomes aware that the error in their interpretation is consistent with their erroneous beliefs and rules, we then work on developing alternative beliefs and rules consistent with their new interpretation of the event or stimulus. It is also useful to have the client maintain a daily journal of negative situations that may occur which includes their feelings, beliefs and rules that they can identify in response to the situations. The daily journal is reviewed each session by the therapist.

Trap Box Exercise

Most criminal justice clients feel trapped in their present lifestyle and have little or no understanding of how or why they feel trapped and are unable to change. I use what I refer to as the trap box which I draw on a blackboard (as shown in Figure 4) so that it becomes visual for the client in order to speed up the realization that any situation, event, stimulus, or risk factor that the client is confronted with and feels helpless changing, or responding to, is largely of their own making. The trap box assists the client in identifying their distorted cognitions, beliefs, and rules and illustrates the fact that three of the four walls within which they feel trapped are self created. The description of each wall and the sentence by which it can be brought into the client's awareness is as follows:

1. Situation/Stimulus/Risk Factor (1)
2. I think that... (client's interpretation of the Situation/Stimulus/Risk Factor) (2)
3. And I believe... (client's belief about the Situation/Stimulus/ Risk Factor) (3) This often parallels the client's interpretation.
4. The way I will handle this event... (client's description of their rules) (4)

Figure 7

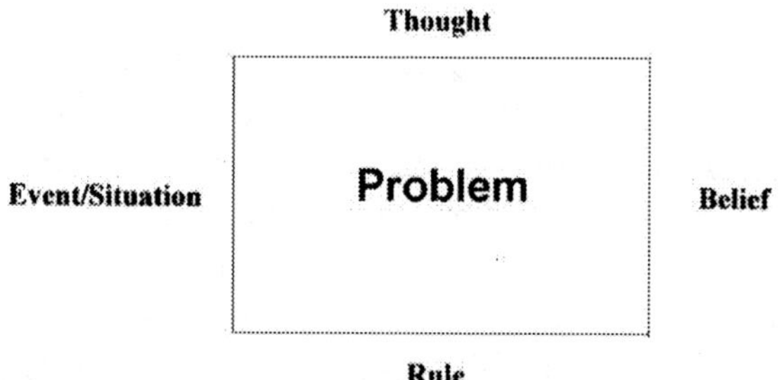

There may be little or nothing a client can do to avoid a high-risk factor or to change a situation; however, they do have the ability and power to re-evaluate their interpretation and beliefs pertaining to the situation or risk factor and make alternative choices. By recognizing that they have the power to do this, they regain control of the situation or high-risk factor and begin the process of removing the walls of the box in which they have trapped themselves. During this exercise the therapist needs to be active and directive if the client gets stuck at one of the walls. The therapist should identify, confront and challenge the client during the exercise with any cognitive distortions, polarization, personalization, over generalizing, discounting or catastrophizing that the client may be doing.

Role Playing

There are both emotional and behavioral components in role playing. When using this technique it is important that the therapist interrupt the client when they identify a distorted belief or rule that is contributing to their life problems and assist the client in changing their distorted belief and rule to an appropriate one. The focus here is to work through the underlying distorted belief and rule that is related to their problem. For example, James has difficulties in his relationships with women because of his belief that he is just like his father, and therefore no woman would really want him. The thought of not being wanted and rejected brings out his feelings of being sad. James would role play a conversation with a woman, acknowledging his feelings of being sad and his distorted belief and rule leading to it and challenge the belief "no matter what I do, I'll never be any different than my father" and the corresponding rule of "don't succeed."

Reverse Role Play

Sometimes I'll engage in a reverse role play with the client. For example, with James I would stubbornly hold on to his belief "no matter what I do, I'll never be any different than my father" and the corresponding rule "don't succeed." James is asked to dispute my belief and rule and try to convince me to reject them. This technique works well because it is James that is describing the irrationality of the belief and rule himself and not the therapist.

Rational Emotive Imagery

In rational emotive imagery, (Maultsby, 1984) clients imagine themselves thinking, feeling and behaving exactly the way they would like to think, feel and behave in real life. This particular technique can also be used to have the client imagine the worst things that could happen to them if they maintain their distorted thought, feeling, belief or rule, and then to change them to ones that are more appropriate that would avoid the negative consequence happening to them. According to (Ellis, A, 1988) if we continue practicing the appropriate rational emotive imagery several times a week for a few weeks we will eventually no longer feel upset over such events. Some clients may have difficulty with maintaining the process of challenging their irrational thoughts, feelings, beliefs and behaviors. One thing the therapist may suggest that will assist the client in maintaining their rational emotive imagery is the development of rational statements they can repeat to themselves at various times during their day. An example might be "I want to have a meaningful relationship because I am not like my father. I don't have to believe that I am like him. I can do this, I can be successful."

Daily Homework

Because of the severity of most criminal justice offender's psychopathologies, their multiple distorted beliefs, rules and other factors that put them at risk of re-offending, I assign to them what I refer to as their permanent daily homework.

Each group member is provided with a supply of forms that outline my modified ABCDE method for identifying and disputing their distorted thoughts, feelings, beliefs, and rules on a daily basis as they encounter unpleasant situations or high-risk factors. The idea is that the client is identifying their own cognitive distortions outside of the group and taking active control of the situation by challenging them and developing alternatives. Each group session requires the clients to share any difficulties they may have encountered in challenging a distorted thought, feeling, belief, rule, or in developing an alternative. The daily homework assignments are later reviewed by the therapist who may identify other distortions or problems that will be addressed in the next group session. Below is an outline of the modified ABCDE method form I use for my group homework assignments.

Homework Assignment

Name: ______________________________
Group: ___________________________
Therapist: __________________________
Date Completed: __________________

Activating Event: Describe in detail the event or situation. Be certain to include WHERE, WHEN, WHAT, WHO, of the event or situation.

____
____
____
____
____
____

Beliefs: Describe in detail what you were thinking. Don't worry about language. State what you were saying inside your head to yourself about the event or situation.

____
____
____
____
____
____

Rules: Describe in detail exactly HOW you would generally approach this type of event, situation, or person.

____
____
____
____
____
____

Consequence: What was the consequence of your belief(s)? Did you feel, sad, mad, scared, confused, guilty? What did you do? Be very specific in describing your feelings and identify as many as you can, as well as your reactions.

____

____

____

____

____

____

Disputes: Identify any and all inaccuracies that you can in the above belief you have about this event or situation. Create an alternative belief about the event or situation.

Use the sentence stems below to help you create an alternative.

A more accurate way of considering this is: ____

____

____

____

____

That's not completely true because: ____

____

____

____

____

A more rational way of approaching this event, situation or person is:

____

Effective Rational Belief(s): Write out a few sentences about how your disputation changed your belief. What solutions did you discover that you weren't aware of before? How did, or will, your behavior change?

____

Bibliotherapy

I have a standard procedure that I follow during the early stage of a group's development. I issue an introductory book on REBT to all my new group therapy clients for them to study between group sessions which make my job teaching the model much easier. During the course of treatment I assign certain reading assignments dependant upon where we are in treatment. By continually giving them reading assignments between sessions, several objectives are achieved:

1. Responsibility rests primarily with the group for their therapy. If they read they will better understand they have alternatives to their distorted beliefs and rules which were previously unknown to them. Generally, those clients that are motivated to change will ask questions and try out new behaviors.
2. Impasses in therapy are more easily observed when the client(s) begin to forget to complete their assignments. For many of the clients in group forgetting is an indicator they are stuck. For some, it may be an indication they are not motivated to change. This needs to be carefully evaluated by the group therapist.
3. Assists in establishing a common therapeutic language that will be used in group.
4. Provides group discussion material.
5. Facilitates self analysis.
6. Expands the clarity of the therapeutic process by providing an educational focus.

The use of bibliotherapy aids me in identifying those clients who are not motivated and may not benefit from being in group. This allows me, if I am unable to motivate the client, to focus more attention to those in the group who are more highly motivated.

Four Chair Work

Through the use of Gestalt techniques, a client can become aware of their distorted cognitions, feelings, beliefs and rules. Sometimes when I identify a client's distortion, situation or event, I set up a four-chair exercise as described below:

Chair 1. Distorted thought, situation or event
Chair 2. Belief
Chair 3. Feeling
Chair 4. Rule(s)

The client begins in chair 1 sharing the identified distorted thought. The client then moves to chair 2 and describes in detail their beliefs about their thought. Once the client describes their beliefs they move to chair 3 and must identify and express their feelings in detail about their beliefs they identified in chair 2. Once this is completed satisfactorily, the client then moves to chair 4 and describes in detail how they would generally approach this type of stimuli. During the entire process the therapist must be active by probing and assisting the client in identifying their beliefs, feelings, rules, and making the connection to their thought, event or situation.

After the client has successfully moved through all four

chairs they move back to chair 1 and work to change the distorted thought to a more rational thought. If it is a situation or event that cannot be changed, the client is asked to make a more rational assessment of the situation or event with the assistance of the therapist, if needed. The client moves to chair 2 and describes their new belief about the alternative thought, situation or event. Then the client moves to chair 3 sharing their feelings, and then to chair 4 describing a more rational approach to dealing with similar thoughts, events, or situations if encountered in the future. Through this Gestalt technique, the client is able to identify their distortions and with the assistance of the therapist give themselves the information they need to correct them.

Provocative change

I have no idea where I came up with this technique; it was probably a result of my own frustration with certain types of clients that are low energy, never get excited about much, and are resistant to making any changes what-so-ever. In using this particular technique I set the client up to become argumentative in defending his right to change whatever they want, including what they believe or feel. Following is an excerpt from a longer group session to give you an idea of how this technique can be used.

Frank: Nikko, you said in our last group session that "the only thing women were good for was sex." Am I correct?

Nikko: Yeah, so what? It's true!

Frank: You know, I've been thinking about that, and here's what I think. I think that a guy like you has absolutely no choice but to believe that because your experience with women hasn't been that extensive, and besides, you're just not smart enough to think and believe anything different. What do you think?

Nikko: I think you're wrong. I'm smart enough to believe whatever I want to believe.

Frank: I doubt that Nikko, because I don't think you're smart enough to be able to think of positive things about women.

Nikko: You're wrong again. I'm smart enough to think of positive things about women if I wanted to.

Frank: I doubt that. Also Nikko, I don't think you're smart enough to want to even try. Let's check it out with the group and hear what they say.

Group: Group members provide feedback in support of my confrontation with Nikko.

Frank: It doesn't sound like many of the other group members think you're very smart either Nikko. What do you think?

Nikko: I think I'm pissed off now. I'm as smart as I want to be. I know of plenty of good things about women.

Frank: I don't know Nikko, I don't know what you know, or if you know anything positive because I just don't think you're bright enough to think anything other than what you already think about women. I guess I would owe you an apology if I was wrong, but I'm smarter than you and I'm not wrong.

Nikko: You're not so smart, I think you're a-----------------------------------, so you can get ready to apologize. I know that women are as smart as men. I know that not all women just want sex.

Frank: That's it. That's all you know? See I'm right, you're not so smart and I don't have to apologize to you. What do you think group? Was that enough for me to have to apologize for thinking Nikko doesn't know much?

Group: Group agrees that Nikko's list of positives wasn't very good.

Frank: Now what Nikko? The group even said you don't deserve an apology yet.

Nikko: Well, I wasn't done yet. I know that women have feelings. I know that most times women are good mothers. I know that you shouldn't hit a girl or a woman. I know that some women work hard like I do. I know that some women are good wives or mates. I know that it can be fun having a woman as a girl friend. I know that they are nurturing, uh, uh, uh, PAUSE.

Frank: You know what Nikko? I do owe you an apology. I was wrong. You are a smart guy. Let me ask you something. Even being as smart as you are, with all the potential you have, that maybe you set it up for people to think you're not very smart because of you hanging onto believing things like that?

Nikko: Sometimes.

Frank: I agree with you. Can you agree with me on this statement? "Having sex with a woman in a meaningful relationship is pleasurable, but women are also capable of contributing other things in your life other than just sex?" As you now know.

Nikko: Well yeah, the right woman could.

Frank: OK, but can you agree that women in general are good for more than just sex?

Nikko: Yeah.

Frank: That's good Nikko. Group time is just about up. Between now and the next group session I want you to think about when and how you came to have such a belief that women are good for only one thing. Write it out on paper specifying when, where, with who, and why and we'll discuss it in group. Good work Nikko.

As I mentioned above, I only use this particular technique when I have a client that is passive, resistant, or is determined they won't change. The above is a short excerpt of the session. Nikko did follow up with his homework assignment and in following sessions he identified and also changed the rules he played by to maintain his belief about women.

Sometimes I set up the provocation to get a client to defend their right to change their thought, feelings, beliefs, rules, or their right to live a pro-social lifestyle. I want to mention that it is important for the therapist to carefully evaluate the client prior to using this technique. It wouldn't be advisable to provoke a client that has a severe anger problem, or has a record of assaultive behaviors unless the therapist is skillful in controlling the dialogue and de-escalating anger and potential acting out.

Some aversive behavior modification techniques can be used to lead the client to analyze and discuss their beliefs about certain events by becoming aware of the negative consequences they may suffer. This opens the door for discussing with the client what thoughts, feelings, beliefs and rules need to be changed in order to avoid the negative consequence. One such method that is administered on an imaginative level is covert sensitization.

Covert sensitization is a verbal aversion technique by which some unpleasant consequence happens as the result of the client doing something illegal. For example, being arrested, incarcerated, or the loss of a relationship is paired with a scene of some deviant behavior such as committing a robbery, molesting a child, raping a woman, stealing a car, or other event. The advantages of this technique are that the client not only becomes aware of the consequence of the negative behavior, but it can also open the door to explore with the client what beliefs, feelings, and rules need to be changed in order to avoid the negative consequences.

Social Skills Training

One of the major goals in treating criminal justice offenders is their development of appropriate social skills. Most offenders come from environments where they lacked appropriate role models and have never been taught interpersonal skills such as keeping eye contact while in a conversation, how to make small talk in social settings, how to ask for what they want, how to say no politely, how to ask for a date, how to resolve a conflict, how to express feelings appropriately, etc. As a result of their lack of social skills they experience difficulties in developing a pro-social support system, making friends, being empathetic, solving problems, and interacting with others. Their lack of social skills results in their becoming isolated and trapped within their antisocial peer culture. The development of social skills also improves the client's self esteem and likelihood that others will respond to them more favorably. Social skills training doesn't need to be a separate activity from the client's assigned group. Social skill development can be incorporated into group therapy sessions.

Some cautions for a therapist to be aware of when teaching a client a new social skill is to be certain that the skills being taught are applicable for the specific client.

It is also critical that the therapist does not overwhelm the client by attempting to alter or change multiple behaviors at one time which could result in the client failing. This failure could reinforce their belief that nothing works for them and that nothing will ever change.

Some specific techniques that are generally used in social skills training include role playing, modeling, shaping, reinforcement and feedback. Preparing the client or group for social skills training requires diplomacy on the therapist's part as clients may be become discouraged by being told they lack social skills. From the client's frame of reference this may be interpreted as "I can't even do that right. On top of everything else, I don't even have the skills needed to live in society. I'm a real loser." The therapist may want to assure the client and group that no one has perfect social skills, even the therapist.

Some target behaviors to consider, depending upon the client's or group's needs, that may be worked on include:

1. Communication skills, apologizing, giving compliments
2. Anger control skills
3. Conflict resolution skills
4. Problem solving skills
5. Emotional management skills
6. Assertiveness training
7. Empathy training and understanding the feelings of others
8. Avoiding physical confrontations
9. Introducing themselves to others, asking for a date, etc.

Empathy Training

Empathy training is one of the most important components of all offender treatment populations including general offenders, sexual offenders, and substance abusers. It is rare that you will ever encounter a criminal justice offender that is totally devoid of feelings and completely lacks the ability to further develop their empathy skills.

The only exception to this may be in the case of a client that is diagnosed as being psychopathic.

Most offenders have little or no idea of how other people perceive them, so a logical first step in developing empathy is being creative in developing methods in group that allows the clients to see how others see them. One technique that I use is referred to as the mirror game. In this exercise each group member takes turns placing their chair in the center of the group. Each group member individually provides the client in the middle of the group with feedback on how they perceive them. The group members are instructed to individually provide everything negative that they know, see, observe or sense about the client in the middle of the group. Then they are instructed to provide the client with everything they perceive as being positive about them. This balance of both negative and positive feedback to the client avoids forced and insincere positive only comments, and lowers the likelihood of the client being mirrored becoming defensive. Once the group has finished mirroring the client, the client then provides feedback to the group as to how they believe they are seen negatively and positively by other people, and what they think they need to change in order to be perceived more positively.

Methods that are utilized to develop victim empathy

include clients writing a letter to the victim stating how they think they have affected their lives by robbing them, stealing from them, sexually assaulting them, or abusing them. Each group member then reads the letter in group getting feedback from the group as to whether it was sincere, what may have been lacking, or what should have been included. Other methods of developing victim empathy in group is to have each group member take turns describing their crime, and as they are describing their offense they write on the blackboard each way they affected their victim's life and how they are feeling at that moment.

Another method is role playing using the gestalt two chair method or fixed role play having another group member or therapist being the victim. A very powerful method of developing victim empathy, that I personally utilize, is psychodrama. However, to utilize psychodrama appropriately requires extensive training and even then it requires strict supervision by the therapist to assure that the client's behaviors are not being reinforced by the re-enactments of their crime.

Anger Management

The recognition and importance of anger as a factor contributing to criminal acting out behaviors, substance abuse, sexual offending, and domestic violence battering as well as other violent offenses should not be ignored in treatment. The chronic and situationally induced anger of most offenders can almost always be traced back to their early life experiences of being a victim themselves, which became a lifelong anger that is ever so often enthused by either real or imagined circumstances. Anger management groups can focus on the client's childhood victimization, and also assist them in developing alternative coping strategies when faced with anger-provoking situations.

The REBT model, as discussed previously, is an excellent anger management tool because it focuses on the client's underlying belief system that creates their distorted emotions and the resulting behaviors. Most offenders will say that the reason they get angry is because either "someone disrespected them," "they were challenged by someone," "they didn't like a situation," or they "felt threatened in some way." Actually none of these situations alone causes the client's anger. According to (Ellis, 1977; Novaco, 1975), anger results from how people view what happens to them. In anger management, the role of cognitions that create the client's anger can be illustrated utilizing the ABC model developed by (Ellis, 1962). For example:

A: Activating event: A friend does not show up when they said they would.

B: Beliefs (self talk that lead to C):

1. They should not have disrespected me like that.
2. I should beat the hell out of them when I see them.
3. I have to get even with them.

Rules: Don't let anyone disrespect me. Don't trust anyone. Don't get close.

C: Consequences (in reaction to A): Emotions: Anger and rage.

Behaviors: Went looking for their friend, shouted using abusive language, hit the other person.

The objective of anger management is to assist the client in replacing their distorted anger and use the energy they use to get angry to solve problems instead. Another objective of anger management is to raise the client's level of frustration tolerance. This can generally be accomplished by using the ABC model along with teaching the client the difference between anger and aggression. Another objective is to assist the client in identifying their distorted cognitions as being the core of their anger problem. The therapist needs to explain to the client that anger is not a bad emotion and that it can be constructive if the energy is used for problem solving, and can also be destructive if used to get even with someone or getting into fights.

Other strategies that can be combined with the ABC model are (a) reading assignments, (b) assisting the client in developing empathy skills using some of the techniques we discussed on empathy, and (c) assisting the client with increasing their motivation to change by having them list on a blackboard the pros and cons of being angry.

Chapter 7: Gender Specific Treatment Needs

(Contributor: Claudia Timmons, MA)

The increase in female arrests, charges, convictions and incarceration is becoming an increasingly important issue. According to the Bureau of Justice Statistics, 2001, the number of females under correctional supervision in the United States rose from 410,000 in 1986 to 895,300 in 1997. Although male and female criminal justice offenders may share many of the same psychosocial problems as discussed previously, the rise in the number of women entering the criminal justice system has raised awareness of the differing needs of women.

The majority of women involved in the criminal justice system dropped out of school at a young age and are undereducated, unskilled and poor. An overwhelming majority of the women are African-American. According to the Bureau of Justice Statistics, 1999, approximately 70 percent of these women have an average of two young children, are single and come from impoverished urban areas. The majority of adult female offenders had their first contact with the criminal justice system as a juvenile. Many times these women were involved a run away in order to escape being physically or sexually abused. For some, this began their involvement in property crimes, prostitution and/or substance abuse. Another complication for the female criminal justice offender is homelessness (Bloom, 1998b).

A recent study (Messina, et al, 2001) indicates that drug-dependent women and men differ radically in their substance abuse problems, psychological functioning, employment histories, sexual and physical abuse histories, criminal involvement, and child support activity prior to their involvement with the criminal justice system. Women are more likely than men to have committed their crime in order to acquire money for drugs. Although some female addicts engage in prostitution in order to support their drug habit, it is more common that they commit crimes such as forgery, burglary, shoplifting or theft.

The correlation between female criminality and substance abuse is significant, with research indicating that females who use drugs are more likely to be involved in criminal activity (Merlo and Pollock, 1995). According to (CSAT, 1997), approximately 80 percent of women in state prisons have substance abuse problems, and according to the (Bureau of Justice Statistics, 1999) approximately 50 percent of female offenders were abusing alcohol or drugs at the time of their offenses.

I asked Ms. Claudia Timmons, someone I have the greatest respect for, to write the following section on what it is like for a female substance abuser and female ex-offender to recover. Claudia is a recovering addict and ex-offender, as am I. Today, she is a powerful therapist and lady who touches many lives and leads other ex-offenders into recovery. The following is Claudia's contribution sharing her personal experiences as an addict, offender, treatment, and recovery in her own words. I think you will find her testimony both encouraging and useful in your work with female criminal justice clients:

It has been said that women "think differently than men." This is true, in my opinion, and although much has been made of these differences when it pertains to intimate relationships, I feel it's important to look at the ways in which women think and feel when those "relationships" involve drugs and/or alcohol. This is also an "intimate" relationship. The drug becomes the user's partner, in every sense of the word, and everyday functions are geared solely towards the acquisition of that drug of choice.

When I was using, I didn't think too much about stopping. There were of course times when I would make feeble attempts at stopping, but I always returned to the drug. It became my mother, father, girlfriend, boyfriend, and child. The drug became my everything. The only time I got away from it was when I was locked up in prison. I used very little in prison – not because I didn't want it, but because I preferred not to get caught up in the "mix" that is inherent in the prison culture, often involving violence. Typically, however, as soon as I got out, my first stop would be a connection close to wherever my release was at the time.

It just seemed like the think to do…my comfort zone that I kept running back to. That trail also led back to prison, which in a sense was also my comfort zone. It was the easy part. Life on the outside is the hard part, at least the "normal" life is. I now tell my clients that once you clean up you will have a whole new set of problems. It's called LIFE. Life entails the so-called "normal" things – bills, rent, mortgage payments, car payments, etc.

What is "normal" to us, as addicts, is not the same thing as what is "normal" to the majority of society. An analogy I sometimes use in group settings when discussing the change of paradigms is to have the group members think of the governor, or a state representative, or even their dentist or doctor. These are usually considered "normal" people (although we sometimes wonder in this day and age). Imagine them surviving just one day of our life when we are in active addiction. Could they do this? Maybe they could, but they certainly could not with the ease that we do. The key word there is "survival."

I truly believe that for an addict to change their life, whether it is a man or a woman, there has to be a "shift from within." There has to be something that initiates the process of change. It can be anything, such as a child, a parent, a concrete table for that matter, but it must be something that becomes higher on the priority list than the drug. For me, I did not want to die in prison and be buried in one of those prison cemeteries that no one cares about. This is how that "shift" happened for me.

I was locked up on one of my many prison violations in California. I had just arrived from the county jail; it was two days before Christmas. Due to the overflow problem that so many prisons contend with, we, meaning the women that came from that particular county jail, were placed in the Ad Seg unit, which just happened to be in the same building as the California Death Row. There were, at that time, seven women on the "Row." They were separated from the rest of us but only by that rust colored mesh caging, so it was easy to talk to them. Ad Seg is typically extremely noisy – people yelling back and forth, "fishing," and all kinds of prison relationships being carried on from behind locked doors. I'm not a very talkative type of gal, especially when I'm sick from heroin withdrawal, so my participation in this chaos was nil. I was experiencing my usual withdrawal, going in and out of a strange kind of consciousness. I remember hearing Christmas music, "Silent Night" to be exact. I also remember thinking that I must be having one of those "kicking" dreams and that none of this was real. So I got up and peeked out of that little 4" x 12" window and saw the Death Row women making a Christmas tree out of paper and a radio beside it. (To clarify, in California the women on Death Row are allowed to have their own TVs, radios, clothes, etc). They were trying to bring the Christmas spirit into Ad Seg, and they were succeeding, because it was quiet in there. No noise at all, except for Silent Night. Right then and there, despite my severe withdrawal, I remember thinking, "What are you doing? These women will never see daylight again, and you have a choice. You don't have to come back in here anymore, you idiot." That moment changed my life. That's not to say that I stopped my drug use immediately, or didn't return to prison a couple more times on violations. But it was the beginning of change for me. That was my "shift," and I've never forgotten it. Some people don't believe this story, and that's okay too, but it's true. And it's powerful, at least for me it is. I hope my experience serves to help others in my work now, as a counselor for those who are heading down the same path as I did. It really doesn't matter if they believe me or not, but I've found that in time they will listen to my story, and identify with it, and hopefully not make it their own.

You may be wondering what all this has to do with treating the female forensic population. Much of what I do is based in the experiential. When I first went in to treatment, I didn't even know what a "group" was. Where would I have learned that – in prison? My first evening in what eventually was the place I learned to be a counselor and help others, I was in a group, but to me it just looked like a big room with some people sitting in a circle talking to me and asking me what my intentions were. I remember the lady who was instrumental in starting this program telling me "you have to detox from prison." Detox from prison? What does that mean? So I just said okay and told them what they wanted to hear. And I kept telling them what they wanted to hear, almost throughout my entire stay. I learned the group process very quickly, and applied my street smarts to this process. I threw something that sounded good out there every once in awhile just to keep them off my back, and that way I wouldn't have to reveal any of that "inner stuff" that I now know was instrumental in keeping me in my addiction. I was so good at this that I became a "demonstrator" fairly quickly, a staff member, teaching and guiding others who were new in treatment. For me, it was a big mistake. I was a hypocrite and soon enough I found myself back in the cooker. And back in prison. I set it all up. It actually took about three or four tries at treatment before I finally started to get it. The program I was in was a therapeutic community. It was very confrontational. I was called everything but "a child of God" at one time or another and this was because I was all those things they said I was. I was ungrateful, had no humility, I had a sense of entitlement, I was condescending. Until I actually learned how to become grateful and humble and didn't feel I deserved anything and that the world was not out to get me I was stuck. This therapeutic community was in prison, twice, and also in the free world.

When I facilitate groups now, I recognize when someone is throwing something out there to pacify me or the other group members. And it is usually a woman doing this. I feel a lot of that has to do with feelings of guilt and shame at not being successful at motherhood. That is just my own feeling. I was not a good mother because of my using, so I'm not an expert on parenting, but I do see that when a woman is addressed on her relationship with her children, she becomes at first defensive, then defiant and angry, and ultimately tearful and emotional. It takes time to come to terms with the guilt and shame that result from the lack of parenting. Often times, the intensity of this guilt and shame results in relapse. I attempt to help people understand that "it's a process, not an event;" they didn't get there overnight so they are not going to heal overnight. But it can be done, and women can successfully reunite with their children, and families.

One of the dynamics of prison life is that the women often cultivate and build a "family" while they are locked up. This is very common. Women have a need for affection and closeness – much more so than men. They need to be able to talk and express thoughts and feelings. It is not unusual to see a "mom," "dad," "daughter," and even "son" in the prison "family." This "extended family" enables a woman to feel, at least to a certain extent, that she is included rather than excluded, and she can, in a sense, replace some of the shame and guilt that comes from not being with her own family. About 85 percent of women in prison are mothers. Out of that 85 percent, only about one to two percent has visits from their children and/or other family members. Sadly, many don't even know where their children are. Women tend to lose touch with their families much more quickly than men once they are in prison.

One of the more progressive aspects of addressing the escalating societal drug problem that inevitably leads to a person, whether it be a man or a woman, excluding themselves or being excluded from their families is the recent implementation of prison drug programs. These programs are typically based on a therapeutic community modality, although in the past decade or so the TC has become much more "dignified." One of the first TCs was Synanon. I have relatives that were in Synanon. In fact, the first time I was ever sentenced to prison I was given a choice – prison or Synanon. I chose prison, and unfortunately, made that my life for many years. Synanon, at first, was a success in many people's eyes because it was a place that afforded a different kind of life and people became part of the program in terms of peers helping peers. I know people today that attribute their continued recovery to the tools that they learned in Synanon. As time went on however, the dynamic changed and it became a more violent and self-absorbed entity.

At Synanon, they called groups "games," and many left after having been confronted in the "game" in a very aggressive and demeaning manner. Synanon eventually became more of a "lifestyle" program, even to the point where addicts were no longer allowed in. The corporation dissolved at the end of the 1980s after the IRS took over. Some of the people who were in Synanon went on to start their own programs, but did so with much more gentleness. Groups, although sometimes confrontational, were no longer aggressive and demeaning, and people learned the difference between "ratting" and "holding accountable." The prison paradigm was beginning to change. Today, some of these more dignified programs are in the prisons. With an 85 percent recidivism rate, mostly due to drug addiction, society and the "powers that be" in the higher echelons of the corrections systems are recognizing the importance of these in-prison programs. This is where a person can, if they are willing to begin to remove the prison mask, begin the lifelong process of change. Of course, a person has to be willing to change, and sometimes this willingness takes years to unfold. In today's treatment world, we are discovering that women are being charged with many of the same crimes that were once attributed to men – murder, armed robbery, domestic violence, and even sexual assaults. The reporting on these crimes however is skewed, at least in terms of numbers and statistics. More males than females are arrested and convicted, and therefore, there are more males than females in out-patient and in-patient programs. The severity of the crimes however is the same. I have gone to significant lengths to coordinate women's groups and men's groups separately in an effort to address the issues from a gender-specific perspective. For example, a woman will talk much more freely about having supported her habit by prostituting herself than a man will. That same woman may have also committed an armed robbery, which she also will talk about. The man who has sold his body for money and who has also committed an armed robbery will openly talk about the armed robbery almost to the point of wearing it as a "badge of honor," but when the subject of prostitution comes up, he will shy away and attempt to re-direct the group. In a setting with other men, that man has way too much pride to admit something like that. My hope in group facilitation is to create a safe sanctuary where a person can say whatever he or she wants to or feels the need to. In doing that, they are making the group safe for others to talk about some of the same things that they previously wouldn't talk about.

The issues that people think they "will take to the grave" are the same issues that continue to hold them hostage and will keep them using. By verbalizing these issues, it takes the power out of them, and gives the client power instead. I feel that group therapy is a very effective tool in recovery. Women are typically more receptive in a shorter period of time, but when a man makes the decision to let go of the pride, the group process becomes a powerful tool for them also.

I have found that many forensic clients have co-occurring disorders that have previously remained undiagnosed. Prisons and jails typically don't have the trained staff needed to treat these disorders, so the clients come to us and are in need of a wide variety of services, both clinical and in the case management realm. In terms of Axis II diagnoses, I don't see an abundance of personality disorders, but they are there, usually in conjunction with an Axis I diagnosis of depression and/or Schizoaffective Disorders. Since the personality disorders for the most part start becoming apparent in earlier years, it is common for the depression or other Axis I disorders to enhance the symptoms of the identified personality disorder. Most of my clients have substance abuse issues to go along with the mental health issues, and they have been self medicating for many years, not even knowing what they are medicating for. Women especially appear to be more susceptible to depressive disorders more so than any Axis II disorders. I approximate that 60 percent of the clients I work with have exhibited symptoms of depression. Out of that 60 percent, approximately 40 percent are female. Sometimes the depression is situational and will subside after about six months of counseling. Sometimes, however, it is clearly a clinical issue and appropriate medications are warranted, although I hesitate to recommend what I feel often becomes a toxic combination of psychotropic drugs due to over-prescribing by doctors. I'm very careful with that aspect of treatment and often request a second opinion from a well-respected clinical psychologist that I've worked with for some time.

Another Axis I diagnosis that I've found to be common is Post-traumatic Stress Disorder (PSTD). This is often based in childhood trauma, but in many cases of female offenders, it is a residual effect of rape and/or domestic violence. The women are at first very hesitant to talk about this. They either have feelings of guilt at having put themselves in precarious situations to begin with, or sometimes they simply have blocked out the incidents, especially if it involves a family member (father, mother, brother, uncle, etc) leading to a possible Disassociative Disorder diagnosis. Once diagnosed, this can be addressed in a number of ways depending on the receptiveness of the individual and the skill of the therapist.

We are also seeing an increasing number of clients who have been deployed in Iraq and/or Afghanistan. We have found a significant level of success in the utilization of a Post Deployment Assessment and subsequent treatment for those clients who have been or will be diagnosed with PTSD as a result of combat issues.

I have found that treating offenders is often shied away from by some therapists. I don't really know why, but I know that it is a passion for me. I'm sure that some of that passion is because I came from that world, but also because of the dire straits that are now the norm in the corrections systems in terms of over-population and less-than-adequate facilities. I like to think that I play a small, but significant, part in alleviating the prison crises by teaching and guiding those who may be headed down the same path as I was. Prison is not "cool," as so many of our younger (and even older) population try to project. Doing time is not that badge of honor that many of my seasoned convicts wear with what they consider pride. To really change the prison paradigm, one must change his or her cognitive processes, and replace negative with positive thinking. There are so many behaviors involved in the prison mentality, most of which people don't even realize they are exhibiting in the free world. They are released from prison, but they're still "walking the yard," even in treatment, if allowed to do so. They are still trying to be that "shot caller." I've seen men and women attempt to take over groups with their "shot-caller" mindset. In an individual session that is much less common because there is an audience of only one, and the "one" in this case, is me, and that won't work with me. The seasoned convict will not sit with their back to the door, so I move them in to a position in a group that purposely places them with their back to the door. When this is done, the "shot caller" will become more vulnerable and receptive to what is being processed in the group – at least that is the hope. When they sit with their arms crossed in front of them, I ask them to sit straighter and uncross their arms. This of course is not at all what is going to "protect" them from the "enemies" that they feel are in the room. One of my favorite things to do in a group with convicts is to do a check in. I go around the group and have everyone talk for exactly two minutes about whatever they want. They can talk about how their week is going, how their family is doing, or whatever they feel like talking about. This check in usually turns out to be subject matter for the group and the group turns out running itself, but it also creates a setting where the person who never wants to talk ends up talking – even when they are resentful about it. That's okay too. We can always talk about those resentments that have kept that person using and locked up. It's not that they are intentionally carrying around all that misplaced anger; it's just that they don't even realize they have it to begin with. It's probably never been pointed out to them, and if so, they probably got angry and immediately adopted that "hardwire response," which is the only response they know. My job, and my hope, is to begin the process of peeling off those layers of anger and pain so that the person within can heal and grow.

When I was first approached about possibly becoming a counselor, I resisted the idea with every fiber of my being. I absolutely could not see myself in that position, and certainly not working with the forensic population, or worse yet, in a prison. So I went through the "why am I here" stage, which lasted about two years off and on. After getting clean and having some clean time under my belt, I couldn't figure out what to do with myself. I've had a lot of training in various arenas so I knew I could make a living, but after working in other fields for a while and consistently voicing my resistance to being a counselor, I found that I still had emptiness inside of me. For an addict, that's dangerous. So I opened up my mind and remembered what I had been taught ("it hasn't worked your way, so try something else") and began the long process of acquiring my hours to obtain licensure. I discovered, not surprisingly, that I felt better about myself and my life when helping others who have been or might be headed down that familiar prison road. Today, I can't see myself doing much of anything else. I've often thought about all the precarious and very dangerous situations that I have put myself in when I was using. The predominant thought that comes to mind is that I'm here to talk about it, when I really should have been very badly hurt or worse. So now that I've replaced the old negative thinking with positive thinking, I've come to terms with my life and what I am here for. I'm here to help others. Healing can happen. We do recover.

Specific Female Offender Needs

Besides the obvious barriers to female criminal justice clients seeking treatment such as the lack of childcare; being stigmatized as an offender; alcohol or drug abuser; and negative reactions by family, friends, and neighbors, women also have different treatment issues than men. It may be true that women share almost the same psychosocial problems as their male counterparts, as discussed previously in this text, however, as Claudia points out, many have a history of being raped or battered, resulting in a post traumatic stress disorder, or a disassociative disorder as well as other problems that male offenders don't experience.

According to some researchers (Pollock, et al, 1990) about 50 percent of female offenders have children, and the importance of having children is one of the primary differences between female and male offenders. The majority of women that are seen in the criminal justice system with children are single-parent mothers raising their children alone as a result of separation, divorce, or the father of the child is missing or unknown, which means the woman must tolerate the largest share of financial, physical and emotional care of their children. When they are separated from their children because of their addiction or incarceration they experience extreme guilt, anger, anxiety, depression, a sense of hopelessness, loss and grief. Whether separation from their children is due to incarceration or child protective services removing them from the home because the mother is involved in the criminal justice system doesn't matter, because maintaining contact with the children or foster parents is difficult if not almost impossible. Dealing with these issues should be a major part of their individual or group treatment.

For the most part, female offenders are seen in the criminal justice system for crimes such as forgery, welfare fraud, shop lifting, burglary, prostitution, and small quantity drug dealing. The majority of these women are young poor minorities, lacking in education, have no job skills, and are poorly prepared for the job market, therefore they have difficulty supporting their children. In counseling, the type of crimes women commit that are economically driven should be taken into account, with a focus being placed on assisting them in taking control of their lives by directing them into educational training programs so they can acquire the necessary skills they need to market themselves and support their children. Counseling should also focus on parenting skills, social skills training, survival training, job seeking skills, resume writing, and personal responsibility.

Claudia also mentioned the women that are on death row in the state of California for murder. Most female offenders feel powerless in their lives, they lack responsibility, are passive, and are under the domination of a male that abuses them sexually, psychologically, physically, or pimps them out for drug money. Many times the man is suffering from a character disorder himself. Many of these women end up on death row or a doing life sentence because they see no way out of the pain they are suffering other than to kill the aggressor (Pollock, et al, 1990). In a study of battered women who killed their abusive spouses or partners, (Brown, A,

1987) it was found that "the injuries suffered by battered women range from bruises, black eyes, cuts, broken bones, concussions, miscarriages, as well as injuries to joints, hearing loss, vision loss, burns, or knife wounds."

Claudia discussed briefly that incarcerated women need to hold onto that sense of family and being a part of a family. An important factor that must be taken into account if you are presently working, or planning to work, with incarcerated female offenders is their inclination to affiliate with pseudo-families in order to deal with the severity of their emotional pains because of their incarceration. It is also important to have a thorough understanding of the occurrence of female homosexual relationships in women's prisons by being aware of the many problems that women face while incarcerated, and to be available to them in order to assist them with such issues.

Another way female criminal justice clients, or incarcerated women, are different from their male counterparts is, as Claudia states, they are in need of the feeling of closeness, warmth and are more emotional. This has been validated by (Pollock, et al, 1990) who states that "incarcerated women are more likely to show their emotions, have mood swings, and develop attachments with other people than do incarcerated men."

About 80 percent or more of all female criminal justice clients have a substance abuse disorder; however, the literature also indicates that about 50 percent of these women also have sufficient symptoms to be diagnosed with another mental disorder. Common examples include borderline personality disorder, anxiety disorders, major depression, schizophrenia, post-traumatic disorder, and attention deficit-hyperactive disorder – all of which they have in common with their male counterparts. The primary difference in co-occurring disorders between male and female criminal justice clients is that male offenders are more likely to be diagnosed with a conduct or antisocial personality disorder, which I personally believe is an inaccurate diagnosis because of professionals' stereotypes "that antisocial personality disorders are only found in men." My experience is that many female offenders also have an antisocial personality disorder, but are not labeled as such. An accurate diagnosis is important, because the diagnostic impression determines the course of treatment and prognosis.

Mental Health Issues

Specific mental health and other issues common to many female criminal justice offenders that need to be addressed in treatment include:

1. Major affective disorder
2. Personality disorder
3. Substance abuse disorder
4. Post traumatic stress disorder
5. Impulse control disorders
6. Suicide risk
7. Eating disorders
8. HIV/AIDS and other STDs
9. Hepatitis C
10. Cognitive functioning disorders
11. Schizophrenia
12. Borderline intellectual functioning
13. Healthcare services
14. Financial assistance

The majority of female offenders will present with a primary substance abuse disorder and multiple co-occurring disorders as well. Although 80 percent of female offenders present with a substance abuse problem, it should be treated separately from their criminal behavior because substance abuse is harmful to the user, while criminal behaviors are primarily harmful to the community. I mention this because substance abuse services, and even mental health services, have a long history of connecting the two as one problem.

Traditionally, the substance abuse problem has been treated while minimizing the criminal behavior. The criminal behavior is generally not addressed or the criminogenic needs of the client. Both issues should be addressed in treatment, because both issues cause trauma and more problems in almost all psychosocial areas of the client's life. The substance abuse coupled with the female offender's antisocial life style increases their need for denial in both areas and creates a sense of uselessness and hopelessness in the female offender's life. As with their male counterparts, cognitive-behavioral group psychotherapy is considered to be best practice in treatment of both the substance abuse and antisocial acting out. Psychological and psychiatric services may also be indicated dependent upon the client's individual mental health needs.

Educational and Vocational Needs

The majority of female criminal justice clients are high school dropouts, have no vocational training, or job skills. Treatment should also focus on:

1. Educational upgrading. If the client has no high

school diploma she should be assisted in achieving a general education diploma (GED).

2. Evaluating the client's vocational interests and assistance in locating a training program. Most vocational training programs for females fall into stereotyped areas such as cosmetology, food services, child care worker, general office worker, or some sort of domestic work. In today's society, these type jobs are not adequate (Pollock-Byrne, 1990).

A much more stable and rewarding employment is needed in order to support themselves and their children. (Pollock-Byrne, 1990) argue that without marketable skills and knowledge these women cannot compete in the labor market and are forced into low-income employment. By placing the female offender in these situations, we make it almost impossible for them to avoid recidivism, because they see criminal activities as an "easy out" of their present life situation.

Parenting Skills

The majority of young women seen in the criminal justice system are mothers of approximately 1.3 million minor children and lack adequate parenting skills to care for them. The majority of these children are cared for by their grandparents or other relative, and approximately 10 percent have been placed in foster care. One component of their treatment should focus on teaching these women how to improve their parenting skills with a focus on:

1. Building a positive relationship with their children.
2. Appropriate disciplining of children.
3. Parent/child communication skills.
4. Developmental age appropriate expectations.
5. Stress reduction techniques for self care.
6. Skills to deal with childhood and adolescent behavioral problems that may arise as a result of parental incarceration or separation.

Counseling should also take into consideration reunification possibilities and the long-term effects separation may have had on the mother and child. Mother/child interventions should be developed if reunification is a goal. Many children of female offenders have developmental difficulties or developmental delays, and may exhibit problems in trusting others, getting close to others, and in their interpersonal relationships with those they perceive as being authority figures. It is estimated that at least one in ten of these 1.3 million children will be arrested, charged, convicted or incarcerated for a crime as a juvenile or adult. Early mother/child intervention can reduce the probability of this occurring.

Parenting groups or classes for female offenders with children needs to be respectful, acknowledging the participants desire to be the kind of mothers they want to be. In most cases, female offenders have had no positive role models for effective parenting because of either family violence, alcoholism, substance abuse, incarceration of their parents, emotional, physical, or sexual abuse.

Chapter 8: Dealing With Difficult Group Members

The most common problem I hear from therapists who counsel with criminal justice clients is how resistant they are: they are in deep denial; they are doing nothing; they are disruptive; they won't participate; and the difficulty, if not impossibility, to keep them focused.

There is no technique or set of techniques that will magically work through all of these issues. Working with all clients that have been court ordered to attend treatment in a group setting can be a real problem. In this chapter we will discuss and describe some techniques for dealing with some of these problems. I'll begin with the problem of denial primarily because most criminal justice clients believe that if they deny something long enough and hard enough that it just simply doesn't exist anymore. This frame of reference is reinforced every time the therapist fails to follow through by not working through their denial.

Denial

Denial is the most archaic of the defense mechanisms which involves the client discounting, minimizing or even ignoring some feature of self, others or the reality of a situation. When a client is in denial their frame of reference is distorted or is inconsistent with reality. By denying, the client reinforces their frame of reference and continues their antisocial lifestyles. A client's denial can be observed in four specific areas to avoid dealing with their problems. I have developed a model of denial that I adapted and modified from (Schiff, 1975) that specifically relates to criminal justice offenders. In my model of denial, denial has four levels which need to be worked through systematically.

The following techniques include some strategies used in motivational interviewing that can assist in breaking the client's denial at different levels. The levels of denial are as follows:

Level 1: Denying the existence of a problem. For example, "I don't have a drug problem," "I didn't do what they said I did," etc. Until the client at least admits that a problem exists there is not very much can be accomplished.

Technique: The use of Motivational Counseling Strategies can assist the client in getting through this first level. This strategy involves engaging the client in a conversation about what their life was like before they started using substances. Questions such as "what plans did you have for your life?" and "how do you think your life would have been different?" are appropriate. The object here is not to resolve any issues, but rather to simply establish the existence of a problem by finding out how their life was prior to their being arrested or using drugs compared to how things are now.

Level 2: Denying the severity of their problem. Most criminal justice clients at this level acknowledge the existence of their problem, but diminish its significance to their present situation. For example the clients make statements such as "it's not a big deal," and "oh well, I'll get over it." It's human nature to ignore a situation or event that is not perceived as being severe enough to deal with or with which to be bothered. The client will need to become aware of the severity of their problem(s) in order for them to become motivated to change.

Technique: At this level, the therapist needs to be familiar with the client's past history such as number of arrests, convictions, incarcerations, divorces, family, children, job history, etc. The therapist must make the client aware of the negative effects their present situation and problem(s) have had on their life and how it has affected self and others by linking the negative effects to losses of freedom due to arrests and convictions, job losses, divorces (if any), effects on children (if any), on other family members, financial losses, cost of attorneys, court fines, career loss, lack of education and vocational training, or health. Many times when the client becomes aware of how their problem has affected themselves, family, children, etc, they become motivated to follow through with treatment and find a solution to their problem.

Level 3: Denying a solution to their problem. Many criminal justice clients that have previously been in counseling and participated in support groups and eventually relapse back into their antisocial lifestyles or substance abuse. They come to believe that their problems are unsolvable. They make statements such as "been there, done this," "I tried that, it didn't work," or, "nothing works," and "It's genetic."

Sound familiar? Well, it's not unusual for criminal justice clients that have been exposed to multiple failed counseling experiences to discount the present counseling experience and minimize the solvability of their problem(s).

Technique: A motivational interviewing technique that can be adapted for this level of denial if the client appears hesitant to discuss a way out of their problem is to rationally analyze what is "good" about their substance abuse or lifestyle along with what is "not-so-good." Most clients are often willing to admit that there are less good things which provide the group therapist the opportunity to discover the irrational beliefs that are supporting the client's problem. This technique serves to reduce resistance and allows probing into the less good things and directs the client into rationally deciding on a solution for their problem. The goal here is to engage the client in rationally weighing both the pros and cons of their substance abuse or antisocial lifestyle. The client then weighs the rational pros and cons of changing their behavior. Most times the client is willing to accept the pros about making a change. Once the client recognizes that solutions are available for their problem(s), it is useful to have the client process with the group what solutions are available. It is also important to gain closure from the client as to what solution(s) they will make use of. Some useful interventions questions that you may want to consider to gain closure are as follows:

- "What are the solution(s) you discovered?"
- "Which of these options are you willing to put into practice?"
- "When will you do that?"

- "How do you believe your life will be different if you follow through with this solution?"

Level 4: Denying their ability to follow through with the solution to their problem.

Many clients that have been exposed to numerous counseling attempts that have failed not only think there is no solution to their problems but they also irrationally believe that even if there is a solution they don't have what it takes to make it work for them. They just deny their ability to change: "Sounds good, but I can't do that," "I don't know about this, I tried this once before," "I know this won't work. I just can't do it."

This denial of their ability occurs most times even though they acknowledge that there is a solution to their problem. Getting through this level of denial is critical. The client's continued denial of their ability to follow through with solving a problem may or may not be real. As I have mentioned in this text many times, criminal justice clients are extremely adamant in wanting to sabotage their treatment. Denying their ability may be just one more way the offender is defending their behavior and lifestyle. Or the denial may be real because most criminal justice offenders tend to be powerless and suffer from low self esteem. Either way, real or unreal, the therapist at this point should focus on identifying any irrational beliefs that the client may have, and on getting the client to take full and indisputable responsibility for following through with the solutions to the problems they themselves identified.

Review with the client the pros and cons of holding on to their problems or lifestyle that was identified in Level 3. Some strategies that you may want to use to get the client to stop denying their abilities are:

Technique: Sometimes I ask a client who was their favorite superhero when they were a little boy. For example, if a client says his favorite superhero was Superman, I then ask him if he believes that Superman would have the ability to solve a problem. The answer of course is almost always, "why of course he does, he's Superman." Once the client agrees that the superhero can do anything, I ask them to close their eyes and imagine they are that superhero working on the solutions to their problems. I instruct them to keep their eyes closed and to only open them when the superhero has successfully solved the problem. Once they open their eyes, I have them share with the group how the superhero solved the problem.

Most criminal justice clients, and in particular APDs, have great imaginations and enjoy getting into therapeutic fantasy work.

The goal here is to box the client in by providing a framework (being a superhero) for the client to think about their irrational belief(s) that they may have about their inability to follow through with their solution(s). Most times they, as their superhero, successfully challenge those beliefs. Once the client has identified their ability to do something, you can get your closure using open-ended interventions such as:

- "How compelling is your confidence that Superman can do X?"
- "How are you going to do X?"
- "When are you willing to start doing X?"
- "Again, how will your life be different?"

- "How will I, the group, and other people know you are doing X?"

Effective therapeutic interventions should be planned so as not to begin below Level 1, denial of the existence of the problem. If the intervention begins below Level 1, the intervention will be ineffective and will result in failure.

Resistance

In traditional group therapy, group members display certain behaviors during the different stages of the group's development. However, in criminal justice groups where all the group members have been court mandated to attend behaviors that have become deep rooted within their personality and are experienced as being "that's who I am," or "that's just the way I am," are problematic and extend beyond the initial stages of the group's development. One of the most unrelenting problems criminal justice clients exhibit during treatment is resistance.

Criminal justice clients show resistance somewhat differently than clients that may be treated in a voluntary treatment group. For the criminal offender, resistance is a conscious repression of their thoughts and feelings resulting from early life experiences which contribute to their criminal thinking. While on the other hand, for clients not suffering from such a severe pathology resistance most times is the result of an unconscious repression of a thought or emotion that may be contributing to the problem for which they are seeking help.

Most therapists view resistance as a negative symptom of

the offender's substance abuse addiction if they have one, or their criminal lifestyle, which will be a barrier to a positive treatment outcome. Viewing resistance as a barrier to a positive treatment outcome by a therapist can, in itself, become a barrier in developing a positive therapeutic alliance with the client, which will result in a negative treatment outcome. However, what is not taken into consideration by most therapists is that within the offender's frame of reference resistance is necessary in order to hang on to the only way of life they know "that's who I am," "that's just the way I am," and "this is all I know." In fact, many offenders don't believe that what they have done is illegal or wrong, and the only problem that exists is that they got caught.

Their thinking is something like this: "I really need a coat but I can't afford this one. I probably shouldn't steal it, but what the hell, the store has plenty of coats and they probably pay less than half of what they charge for them. What rip offs they are, they deserve to lose a few coats." When caught, they then perceive themselves as being a victim of the system and not the victimizers.

Many offenders also perceive what they do as just being a normal part of their daily lives "that's just the way I am," and "everyone else does it." Criminal justice clients may resist treatment for a number of reasons:

1. They may perceive themselves as being victimized because they are mandated to attend.
2. They don't believe that the therapist can be trusted because of limited confidentiality.
3. They may believe that counseling/group therapy is for mentally ill persons only.
4. They don't think they have a problem.

5. They are fearful of what may happen if they reveal too much about themselves because of limited confidentiality.
6. They may have concerns or be fearful of how their street peers will perceive them.

The most effective way to deal with the criminal justice client's resistance to counseling or being in group therapy is to deal with it openly and honestly. The therapist should be aware that whenever someone is coerced to comply with something, and threatened with a negative consequence if they refuse, there will be some level of resistance. In this sense, resistance is healthy. In the case of a criminal justice client, the threat of a negative consequence is further intensified once they discover that they don't enjoy the same rights to privacy as non-mandated clients, and that in their case there is only limited confidentiality. These two factors (a) being coerced into treatment, and (b) their limited confidentiality presents a huge problem for a therapist to overcome. When you take these two factors into consideration you realize that under these circumstances they have good reason to feel threatened, for limited confidentiality does not encourage a sense of security and trust.

Resistance on the part of a criminal justice client should be respected and not automatically come to imply that they are unmotivated. Some are unmotivated to make any kind of change whatsoever, but the overwhelming majority is uncomfortable enough in their present life situation to be open to making changes that will improve their life position. The first step toward developing trust and working through the client's resistance is the therapist and client exploring the issues of trust and the client's irrational beliefs about their resistance.

The therapist should make use of motivational counseling approaches to avoid any further resistance and dissolve the existing resistance that may be preventing the client from working on their treatment issues and recovery. The first step in working through the client's resistance is to understand its possible causes. If you don't understand the client's motivation to be resistant ask them. Actual behavior is important. In this case it's resistance, but equally as important are the reasons behind the behavior. Most clients are very willing to discuss why they are reluctant to participate. Seek understanding as to how the client perceives themselves, the problem of being coerced into treatment with limited confidentiality, and you. Once you attain this understanding, use these views to frame interventions for goal-oriented solutions that will influence the client's resistant behavior.

Interventions should be designed in such a way that the client has the opportunity to use their own initiative as much as possible. In order for interventions designed to dissolve resistance to be effective the client must:

1. Believe that their resistance is jeopardizing their recovery.
2. Believe that the severity of their substance abuse or criminal behavior is serious in terms of economic difficulties, incarcerations, and harm to self, family, and others.
3. Believe the pros for changing outweigh the cons.
4. Believe that changes are possible and within their reach.
5. Believe that their present offense is serious enough for them to want change.

Asking clients open-ended questions will assist you in understanding the resistant client's frame of reference, thoughts, feelings and beliefs about what they are resisting.

Asking open-ended questions elicits a dialogue because they generally cannot be answered with just yes or no responses and they encourage the client to speak and participate and keep communication moving. Such interventions may include:

- "How important is it to you to change your present lifestyle?"
- "How important is it to you to change your substance abuse?"
- "How important is it for you to have a better life?"
- "How important is it for you to have your family trust you?"
- "How confident are you in yourself to change X?"
- "How would changing X change your life?"
- "How is X scary for you?"
- "What would it take for you to change X?"
- "What would keep you from changing X?"
- "What is the worse thing that could happen if you X?"
- "What is the best thing that could happen if you X?"
- "What do you need in order for you to do X?"
- "What is the scariest thing about X for you?"

Effective interventions can also assist in identifying the client's irrational beliefs, feelings, and distorted thoughts pertaining to the reasons for their resistance which the REBT model will be useful in challenging and restructuring.

Another technique you may want to use is to have the client write out the pros and cons of not changing, while avoiding labeling the target behavior or situation to be changed as being a problem which may cause the client to become even more resistant.

Most clients will acknowledge the cons of their situation or behavior being targeted for change which can serve to lower their resistance. Once the client responds, this technique allows for group discussion of what is good and what is bad about a situation or behavior being targeted in more detail. The goal is to get the client to share and explore both the pros and cons with the intention of reducing their resistance.

Sometimes having a client imagine what an ideal life would be like for them by having them explore and describe the behaviors that would be required in order for them to have that ideal life. This technique allows for the exploration of the client's actual values and the inconsistencies between their ideal life and the life they are presently living. For some clients, becoming aware of these inconsistencies motivates them to make changes.

For most criminal justice clients, not changing their behavior or lifestyle is more difficult than changing. Most clients will get through this initial resistance and change. Only time will tell on whether they will do so in a positive direction or not, given the severity of their psychopathologies.

Doing Nothing

Every therapist working with the criminal justice population knows how difficult it can be to motivate a client or the whole group to move from doing nothing to doing something. "Doing nothing" can be accurately defined as the lack of a cognitive or behavioral response to an external stimulus, which requires little or no reality testing as to possible consequences. For example, clients do nothing when they fail to participate in the group, fail to complete their homework assignments, "no call, no show" for sessions, or don't follow through with their treatment plan objectives and goals. The client that is doing nothing has three main objectives: (a) making fools of the therapist, (b) sabotaging treatment, and (c) maintaining their belief system (Deisler, 2002). A member like this may have thoughts and feelings such as:

1. "If I say nothing, they won't find out anything about me."
2. "I have to be here, but I don't have to tell them what I think."
3. "This therapist is the same as my probation officer, trying to get something on me."
4. "It's nobody's business what I think, feel, or believe."
5. "If I don't do anything they will get fed up with me and let me out of here."
6. "I'll just play dumb and they'll think I can't do better."
7. "Why should I trust this therapist? They will tell my probation officer everything."
8. "If I say anything, everyone will think I'm a punk or snitch, and no one on the streets will have anything to do with me."
9. "I don't have any problems. The only problem I have is being here."

The therapeutic task for the therapist is to at least get the client moving from doing nothing to doing something by verbalizing these thoughts and feelings. Verbalizing their feelings can assist in identifying their distorted thoughts and beliefs which will allow for further exploration and cognitive restructuring. For example, if the client verbalizes that they can't trust the therapist and that the therapist is out to get them like their probation officer, the client can be asked to describe how they are alike and what convinces them they are alike. The client who thinks -- "I don't have any problems. The only problem I have is being here" – could be allowed to express their anger about being coerced into treatment without interruption from the group or the therapist. If the client complies this may be the very first time that anyone, from the time of arrest to conviction, respected them enough to hear what they have to say and could be the first step in developing a positive therapeutic alliance. Once the client expresses their anger or resentments about being coerced into treatment, the therapist could respond empathically, "I think that I can understand your reasons for being angry and resentful. I would also feel that way if it were me. Now that you have talked about your anger and resentment, what can you do about them?" An intervention such as this moves the client away from just moaning and groaning about their situation into a thinking- and problem-solving mode.

Another approach with "doing nothing" type of clients is to meet with them individually for three or four sessions to further explore their resistance to doing something. This allows both the client and therapist to get to know each other better and assists in developing a positive therapeutic alliance.

Another technique that can be tried as a last resort is to allow the client to do nothing. I will usually allow a client to not participate in group by having them move their chair outside the circle and face away from the group as a natural consequence of doing nothing. This becomes their permanent position until they decide to do something and participate fully in their group. However, I only allow this for four to five sessions while I continually assess the client's needs. If the client fails to respond by no later than the fourth session, I transfer the client to either a psychoeducational group or a task group. If this final effort fails, the client is allowed to experience the natural consequence of their behavior by being terminated and referred back to the criminal justice system.

Defensiveness and Avoidance

Both defensiveness and avoidance are resistant behaviors that criminal justice clients will exhibit to some degree. The difference between defensiveness and avoidance, at least with most criminal justice clients, is defensiveness is most often experienced by the therapist when the client is anticipating something and is prepared to respond in a manner that is designed to prevent the therapist from gaining any information or therapeutic advantage because the client feels threatened in some way. Most times defensiveness takes the form of the client challenging the therapist. While avoidance tactics are more often designed by the client to avoid responding honestly or doing something or preventing something from actually happening. Most criminal justice clients are masters when it comes to avoidance. Both defensiveness and avoidance requires immediate attention by the therapist.

Clients use avoidance techniques such as qualifying their

responses to the therapist's interventions which require a "yes" or "no" response with "could be," "maybe," "possibly," "I don't know," "I'll try," "we'll see," etc. The purpose for these types of responses most times is to avoid making a commitment to do something, sabotaging the therapist or group, or to sabotage their own treatment. Some possible strategies to assist the client in being precise or making a commitment could be as follows:

- "That question required a yes or no response. What are you protecting by responding with maybe?"
- "My question required a yes or no response. You responded with "I don't know." What do you think would happen if you did know and responded yes or no?"
- "My question required a yes or no response. You responded by saying "we'll see." Would you go around the group and tell each person what you think or believe we'll see if you respond with a yes or no?"
- "I'm not clear about your answer. Would you be willing to go around the group and ask each group member if they have a clear understanding of your response?"
- "How about going around the group and completing this sentence as you look each group member in the eye: "One of the ways I keep myself from making any changes by being non-committal is ..."

Another avoidance strategy that is commonly exhibited by clients is generalizing and over-generalizing. Generalizations include such statements by the client as "everyone does it," "my crimes aren't as severe as the others in here," "everyone in here is careful not to share too much." Over-generalizing includes statements such as "Who am I?" "What is the meaning of life?" "Am I really loved?" "What is normal?" Such questions are so overwhelming that no rational thinking person could possibly answer them.

It is useful for the therapist that may have a client that uses generalizations to avoid therapeutic work to develop strategies and design interventions to assist them in becoming more accurate by not making general statements and to focus on themselves, for example:

Client: No one trusts anyone in this group.

Therapist: If you were more trusting in group, what would you say or do?

Client: Everyone I know does it.

Therapist: What would be different for you if you didn't do it?

Client: What I did is not as bad as what everyone else in this group did.

Therapist: Would you tell the group how you think you're better than them?

The Overly Compliant Client

We have all, at one time or another, worked with a client who was a pleasure to work with. Whatever was asked of them, they did it. Every intervention we designed for them resulted in closure – every time. Over compliance, most times, can be a problem because many court-mandated clients are very anxious and eager to please. However, compliance needs to be carefully assessed by the therapist in order to determine if it is real or whether the client is over-adapting and figuring out what the therapist wants in order for them to successfully complete their treatment program and to be released from probation. "Over-adaptation can be easily confused with adaptation which is thinking something through and then deciding to comply because it makes sense to do so (Schiff, 1975)." The difference between over-adaptation and adaptation is over-adaptation is conning. (Schiff, 1975) describes over-adaptation as "psyching out what they think others want of them and adapting to this fantasy."

After a careful assessment if the therapist determines that the client is over-adapting and conning, the over-adapting behaviors can be used therapeutically by the therapist if it is within the therapist's awareness. If it is within the therapist's awareness and is used therapeutically, then unknown to the client it is no longer a con. The client's over-adaptation can be used initially to have the client practice new behaviors which they may eventually adapt to because it makes sense for them to do so. I generally select one behavior at a time for the client to practice. Then, at each group session, I have the client present their appraisal of the new behavior they are presently practicing. This appraisal allows the therapist to possibly identify and challenge any irrational thoughts, feelings, beliefs, or attributions the client may have pertaining to the new behavior, thereby modifying the appraisal. By using the client's over-adaptation strategy in service of their treatment goals, many times the client will become comfortable with the therapeutic process, and what was once acting becomes real.

The Tough Guy

Every now and then the forensic counselor is going to encounter a "tough guy" in their group. Theoretically this shouldn't happen if you have established ideal client criteria for your group and a screening process for admitting new clients into a group.

However, given the severity of pathology many criminal justice clients have some will con their way through and slip through the cracks. When this does occur it presents the therapist with a dilemma because the "tough guy" presents a barrier to the development of the group and can negatively influence the attitude of the whole group.

The "tough guy" is generally disruptive to any therapeutic work being done. They will constantly challenge the therapist on anything and everything in their attempt to make a fool of the therapist. They will not comply with the group rules, will covertly threaten other group members so they will not confront them, will rarely participate in group, and when they do participate they monopolize the group's time. The "tough guy" is like a knight in armor, nothing that is said or done to them seems to penetrate their armor or make a difference.

The dilemma the therapist is faced with is what to do with this type of client. If all traditional therapeutic approaches have been exhausted, including motivational techniques, terminating the client and referring them back to court is a tough decision which must be considered. However, referring a client back to court could have a negative effect on the group's level of trust, and could discourage group participation. It also reflects on the therapist's credibility with the group, and makes them appear as being part of the system. Therefore, the negative effect of the "tough guy" on the group as a whole must be considered against the possible negative consequences of client termination. Termination and referral back to the criminal justice system should be a very last resort.

Because I have a responsibility to facilitate insight into a client's behavior and assist in their growth, I do at times, as a very last resort, utilize nontraditional approaches that are designed to provide a "tough guy" the opportunity to at least become compliant. I have found it difficult, if not almost impossible, to motivate a client unless there is at least a minimal level of compliance. Working with court-referred clients makes the therapist an agent of the court. With that comes a certain amount of power whether we are willing to admit it or not. The therapist has the power to demand behavioral compliance or sent the client back to jail, back to probation, court, etc. Sometimes when the therapist demands behavioral compliance attitude change will follow. John Erlichman once stated, "when you have them by the balls, their hearts and minds will follow (Friedman, 1989)." After everything else has failed, there are some nontraditional techniques that I have used to deal with the "tough guy" that may penetrate their armor will be discussed. However, I want to make clear that clients who are at risk of becoming violent or have a history of violence may not be appropriate for these techniques. This is something that must be carefully assessed by the therapist.

The perceptions you have about the client after your assessment is your best tool in selecting a technique or strategy to deal with their problematic group behavior.

The "tough guy" obviously has an image that they are protecting. The most common response to almost every intervention that the therapist hears from the "tough guy" is,

"I don't know." After a sufficient number of "I don't know" responses, which is usually the fifth, I ask the client to leave the group and stand facing the wall or a corner until they figure out what they do know. I instruct the client that until they figure out what they do know the corner is their permanent spot for every group session. I also instruct them that when they figure out what they do know to take their place in group and share it with the group. Most times the "tough guy" will respond that there is no way that they will comply with this. At this point I give the client a choice, comply or return to the court or probation department for non-compliance and possibly face revocation and incarceration. In almost 30 years of practice I have encountered hundreds of "tough guys," and only two out of those hundreds chose to be referred back to court. I guess they were really "tough guys." Real "tough guys" don't stand in corners or face walls. If the client responds positively and does go to the corner, it is important to stroke them, letting them know that they made the smart choice, and that they have the ability and intelligence to make the right choices when they choose to think something through. It's almost impossible to hold onto their "tough guy" image after their armor has been penetrated. Most times, the "tough guy" does little more than to be compliant after returning to the group from the corner. Some compliance, no matter how little, is at least a start for the client to become motivated.

"Tough guys" that are disruptive in group, covertly threaten other group members, and are not responding, present a more serious problem for the therapist. Because therapists have a responsibility to the whole group, they may have to be firm and refer the disruptive client back to court. For me, personally, this has always been a very last resort.

Most times I will transfer the client to a psycho educational or focus group first, and continue to assess their responsiveness to motivational interventions and readiness to return to a treatment group. If these efforts fail and the client continues to be disruptive, they are terminated and referred back to the court or probation department.

Client Closure

Some clients are very adamant when it comes to thinking of ways to not do anything by monopolizing group time, making a fool of the therapist, or avoiding making changes in their lives. One of the ways some court-mandated clients achieve their goal is by getting stuck whenever their therapist asks them something, or by presenting an issue to be worked on that may or may not be real. I have observed some therapists deal with the impasse and spend the entire group attempting to assist a client in figuring out what they were angry about, fearful of, what they were feeling, etc, without a resolution.

There are many reasons why the therapist shouldn't spend all, or a large part, of group time with a client when it appears there is no solution to the problem. The first reason is that we have a responsibility to the entire group. The second reason is that if the issue isn't real the group will sense that, and in effect, the therapist was made a fool of by their failure to gain closure. If the issue is real, it is the client's responsibility to figure it out – not the therapist. A technique that can be used to get a client thinking and to break through their impasse if it is real, or to cut across a client's gamey behavior if it is not real, is to place it back on the client. For example:

Client. I'm really angry tonight.

Therapist: What are you angry about?

Client: I'm not really sure why, I just am.

Therapist: How do you think I can assist you in figuring out what you are angry about?

Client: I'm not sure.

Therapist: It sounds to me as though you got yourself stuck and now you're unsure about a few things. How about you take some time and figure out what you are angry about and how you can stop being angry. When you have that figured out, let me and the group know before the session ends. Will you do that?

Client: I'll do my best.

If the issue of anger is for real the client may have some concerns about expressing their feelings by being unsure. If so, this needs to be explored further by using one of the following techniques:

- "When you were a child, who told you that it wasn't okay to be angry?"
- "Go around the group, imagine and verbalize what you think each member would think if you were to express your anger."
- "What would your parents say about you being angry?"
- "Whose voice do you hear inside your head when you do express your anger?"
- "Would you be willing to share with the group what it feels like to keep yourself from expressing your anger?"
- "Would you tell the group what you think would be the worst thing that could happen if you expressed your anger?"

- "What do you find particularly disturbing about being angry?"

Another technique the therapist could use is to give the client permission to explore what they believe it would be like for them and the group if they were to express their anger. It's possible that they may fear they will harm someone, totally lose control of themselves, or be misunderstood by others. These detailed fears and issues allow for further group exploration of the client's belief system and cognitive restructuring.

Chapter 9: After Care and Relapse Prevention

Treatment programs end but recovery for criminal offenders, substance abusers, domestic violence batterers, and sex offenders is a life-long process. Many criminal justice clients often need more support than they get from participating in a support group after their termination from treatment. However, participation in a support group is critical for the offender seeking recovery because the group offers support, information, and role models in a non-judgmental environment. Alcoholics Anonymous members help each other to attain and maintain their sobriety, as does Narcotics Anonymous and other groups. One organization that is offender specific is the U.S. Offenders Anonymous 12-step program. For information on U.S. Offenders Anonymous and how to set up a chapter, contact the National Association of Forensic Counselors at www.nationalafc.com.

Aftercare is an inaccurate description because a comprehensive aftercare process should begin while the offender is in treatment. Effective aftercare requires a continuum of comprehensive services in order to prevent the recurrence of criminal acting out behavior that includes intervention strategies and community management. The most effective offender aftercare programs that have lower rates of recidivism requires the offender to attend an aftercare group twice a month designed to target specific dynamic and criminogenic characteristics that are dynamic and amenable to change. The aftercare group also provides the offender with the opportunity to discuss any problems they may be having in adjusting to a pro-social lifestyle or working their relapse prevention plan. It also allows the trained aftercare counselor to identify possible signs of relapse for early intervention.

Community management of the criminal justice client refers to the control of the client while they are on probation or parole. Community management activities include contact with supervising agents, random urine analysis testing for illegal substances, employment verification, electronic monitoring, and halfway house residence. According to (Sherman, et al., 1997), increasing the surveillance of offenders "will prevent criminal activities by reducing both their capacity and their opportunity to commit crimes. Additionally, it is expected that the punitive nature of the sanctions will act as specific deterrence to reduce the offender's future criminal activity."

Developing Interagency and Criminal Justice System Collaboration

The success or failure of any criminal offender treatment program can be directly traced back to the relationship the treatment agency has with the referring criminal justice system. The most effective programs have a working relationship with the client's probation or parole agent from the beginning of treatment right through the aftercare process. In order to reduce the risk of re-offending, and for aftercare to work, there must be interagency cooperation that transcends traditional mental health and criminal justice boundaries.

The treatment agency from which the client was terminated from must also attempt to reconnect fragmented human service agencies in order to provide integrated services to offenders such as employment assistance, vocational training, education, medical care, dental care, vision care, housing, food stamps, WIC, etc. Developing an aftercare program with support from other agencies requires contacting and gathering the cooperation of the decision makers and workers from each agency.

The successful treatment aftercare program for offenders should be thought of as a continuum of care consisting of five parts which include:

1. Aftercare preparatory planning during the client's treatment.
2. Participation of aftercare staff and the client's probation or parole agent.
3. Long-term aftercare activities that will make certain of adequate service delivery.
4. Community management.
5. Interagency collaboration.

Relapse Prevention Plan

Most criminal justice offender programs do not have a formal, structured relapse prevention program that coordinates services for successful relapse prevention. This situation in itself is one of the primary reasons so many offenders re-offend after termination from their treatment program. Approximately 75 percent of offenders seen in treatment that have no relapse prevention plan or strategy will relapse within the first twelve months. A relapse prevention plan along with aftercare services would no doubt reduce this relapse rate dramatically.

During the course of treatment relapse prevention is taught. The offender, whether they are a substance abuser, general offender, batterer, or sex offender identifies the sequence of events (e.g. first thinking about committing an offense, planning an offense, rationalizing the planned criminal behavior, placing oneself in a high-risk situation to commit the offense, and finally committing the offense). Relapse for the criminal justice client regardless of the charge is defined as a single occurrence of a criminal act. A lapse for the criminal justice client is defined as a single event of deliberately placing themselves in a high-risk situation that could result in their re-offending. If the client is taught how to identify the lapses that could lead to a relapse, a full relapse is less likely. Certain situations are more likely to lead to a relapse. For example, a recovering addict choosing to socialize with a substance abuser not in recovery, a recovering sex offender being around small children, a recovering batterer drinking and fighting with his spouse, being bored, being angry or lonely, or using substances which reduce inhibitions are all defined as high-risk situations. During the course of treatment the offender should be taught how to identify their own personal high-risk situations and behaviors and develop a plan to cope with strategies to avoid them. For example, if a recovering child molester wanders into a park where there are small children this would be a high-risk situation for them. The coping strategy or plan may be to immediately leave the park, however, the offender is now aroused. A further plan or strategy may be to contact his therapist, probation officer, or whoever he may have included in his plan that he can contact in such high-risk situations. Part of relapse prevention is to also have the offender maintain a daily journal where they can monitor their own thoughts, beliefs, and feelings as a way of having them identify their irrational beliefs about the high-risk situations they encounter as well as their negative thoughts and emotions which may occur before they commit an offense. The offender in recovery could also carry with them index or reminder cards with cognitive and behavioral reminders such as: "This does not have to be tragic, I am in control." "Because I slipped doesn't mean I have to offend." "I can stop right now if I so choose to." "The consequences would be negative for me if I choose to offend." The process of developing a relapse prevention plan for offenders includes the following:

1. Identifying their high-risk situations that lead to their offending.
2. Identifying their offense patterns and offense cycle.
3. Identify victim preferences, i.e., women, children, males, females, age preference, type of place they prefer to rob or steal from, etc.
4. Sex offenders must identify their deviant fantasies.

5. Developing countermeasures for coping with the identified high-risk situations.

Some high-risk situations that could result in relapse include:

1. Frequenting bars and strip clubs.
2. High-risk employment.
3. Job stress.
4. Marital problems.
5. Planning an offense.
6. Needing excitement or drama.
7. Feeling of hopelessness.
8. Anger, arguments.
9. Loneliness, boredom, depression.
10. Involvement in a dysfunctional relationship.
11. Not taking prescribed medications.
12. Alcohol or drug abuse.
13. Sex offender being near schools, parks, or places where children congregate.
14. Sex offender masturbating to deviant fantasies.
15. Sex offender with sexual pre-occupation.
16. Sex offender's use of pornography.
17. Denial, minimization, rationalization of here and now problems.

The above are just a few of the more common high-risk factors that are usually identified; however, each offender may have other risk factors than those identified above. During treatment the offender is required to identify the sequence of problems and behaviors that have led to their criminal acting out, and then recognize how those problems and behaviors could sabotage their recovery. The client then develops a list of their high-risk factors, explores and develops a coping skill to deal with each of the risk factors that could result in their relapse. Risk factor management involves avoiding those situations that trigger the urge to offend by modifying their behavioral response to the situation and then challenging their irrational thoughts, beliefs, and feelings about the high-risk situation. The offender should be able to challenge their initial thoughts that could lead to relapse on the cognitive-affective level, recognizing that the way they think affects the way they feel and eventually behave. The road to recovery and improved self-worth for the offender is behavioral change. While in treatment, the client should be taught how to analyze their high-risk situations so they can make the link between what is happening, what they are thinking about what has happened, and what they are feeling when they have that thought, and then develop a realistic strategy to deal with it. Relapse prevention planning also involves the development of pro-social recovery activities to assist the client to recognize and cope with their risk factors and warning signs as they progress though their recovery. Each warning sign must have a scheduled recovery activity.

The relapse prevention plan should be updated monthly for the first three months the offender is in aftercare, then quarterly for the remainder of the year, and then once a year thereafter. During the course of treatment only about 20-25 percent of the risk factors and other variables that cause relapse are identified. Therefore, aftercare is necessary for effective relapse prevention.

Updating the relapse prevention plan involves:

1. Reviewing the risk factors, warning signs, coping strategies.
2. Updating the relapse prevention plan to include new risk factors and warning signs identified during aftercare.
3. The development of new coping strategies for the newly identified risk factors or warning signs.
4. Revising and linking the new pro-social activities to the newly identified risk factor or warning sign.

Offender recovery can be defined as a return to a pro-social lifestyle. Relapse is defined as the process of returning to an antisocial lifestyle, re-offending, or a return to chemical use. Relapse is not an event, and does not just happen. It is a process that is progressive with increasing psychological and social distress that leads to the eventual relapse. According to (Gorski, T.T, 1990) recovery and relapse are related processes. To fully understand the progression from recovery to relapse it is also important to understand the dynamic interaction between recovery and the relapse process which is a modification of the Cenaps Model developed by (Gorski, T.T, 1990) to fit criminal justice offenders, sex offenders, and batterers as follows:

1. Abstaining from antisocial peers and activities that support an antisocial lifestyle and developing a support system that supports a pro-social lifestyle.
2. Being aware of painful, irrational thoughts, beliefs and feelings that contribute to self-defeating behaviors.
3. Not using alcohol or drugs.
4. Effectively managing feelings and emotions.

5. Changing criminal thinking patterns that result in self-defeating behaviors and offending.
6. Changing the frame of reference (rules, values, beliefs, morals) about oneself, others and the world.
    1. When a client is progressing towards relapse, this process is reversed:

1. They return to those persons, places and things that support an antisocial lifestyle.
2. They discount or ignore painful and irrational thoughts, beliefs, and feelings that have contributed to their dysfunctional lifestyles.
3. They begin to abuse alcohol, drugs or both.
4. They no longer manage their feelings and emotions effectively by avoiding them.
5. They return to criminal thinking and offense planning.
6. They convince themselves that they, others and world are really not OK.

As in the Cenaps Model the relapse process begins at Step 6 and proceeds upward. For example, let's look at a sex offender and see how a relapse may occur. An offender in recovery becomes frustrated because of the social limitations placed on them being on a sex offender registry. The neighbors don't want them living next to them and employment opportunities are limited because of the registry. They start thinking about how unfair the system is to have done this to them and the reaction they get from others. He begins to feel bad about himself and thinks there is no hope (step 6). He feels victimized and starts planning to get even (step 5). He offends by molesting a child he began grooming that made him feel better about himself (step 4). He begins to worry about being caught and the possible consequences of his behavior. He begins going to bars and drinking again (step 3). As the weeks go by he worries less about getting caught, but intentionally avoids thinking about any consequences, and begins thinking, "well I got away with that offense and I know I can get away with others" (step 2). After re-offending again, he begins to hang out in places where he knows other offenders that have molested children (1).

Support Groups

As (Gorski, 1990) stated, "Relapse-prone patients cannot recover alone. It is the therapist's responsibility to involve significant others in the structured process of relapse prevention planning. Family members, 12-step program sponsors and employee assistance program counselors are significant resources who need to be involved." These concepts not only apply to alcoholics or substance abusers, but also to every criminal justice client regardless of the type of crime committed.

Any part of a relapse prevention plan should require attendance at a support group in order to maintain recovery. If the client is an alcohol or drug abuser, attendance at Alcoholics Anonymous or Narcotics Anonymous should be part of the plan. Many times when a substance abuser or alcoholic is faced with a high-risk situation that could result in relapse, their coping strategy, or escape strategy to avoid relapse is attending a meeting.

Part of the problem for sex offenders is that they have no specific support group they can attend for support to continue their recovery. If faced with a high-risk situation they may have a few contact numbers they can call, however, most sex offenders feel embarrassed or ashamed and don't call.

A new organization that is based upon the 12 steps of Alcoholics Anonymous is Offenders Anonymous where general offenders, sex offenders, and batterers can all attend. One of the rules of OA is that no offender can ever divulge the nature of their crime to other members. Their reasoning for this is two-fold. First, it avoids the criminal hierarchy of crimes. In other words, in the street subculture, an armed robber has more status than a burglar; the burglar has more status than a forger, etc. Second, it provides a safe place to share problems of recovery, and barriers to recovery. It also makes it a safe place for sex offenders who in the street subculture are at the bottom of the hierarchy. OA works on the same principal as AA and NA which contains references to God and a Higher Power. Participation in OA also requires working the steps and sponsorship. Information about OA can be obtained from their web site at www.usoffendersanonymous.org or at www.nationalafc.com.

References

Allen, L.C., MacKenzie, D.L.; and Hickman, L.J. (2001) The effectiveness of cognitive behavioral treatment for adult offenders: a methodological, quality-based review. International Journal of Offender Therapy and Comparative Criminology. 45, 4, pp. 498-514.

Beck, A.T. (1975) Cognitive Therapy and the Emotional Disorders. New York: International Universities Press.

Beckman, L.J. (1980) An attributional analysis of Alcoholics Anonymous. Journal of Studies on Alcohol. 41:714-726

Bloom, B. (1993) Incarcerated Mothers and Their Children: Maintaining Family Ties. In American Correctional Association (Ed.), Female Offenders: Meeting Needs of a Neglected Population (pp. 60-68). Laurel, MD: American Correctional Association.

Brown, A. (1987) When Battered Women Kill, The Free Press, New York.

Bureau of Justice Statistics (1999) Women Offenders.

Center for Substance Abuse Treatment (1997) Substance abuse treatment for women offenders: Guide to promising practices. TAP #23. Rockville, Md.: U.S. Department of Health and Human Services, Public Health Services, Substance Abuse and Mental Health Services Administration.

Corey, G. (2000) Theory and Practice of Group Counseling. 5th ed. Belmont, California: Brooks/Cole.

Drury, F.L. (2000) Offender Barriers to Recovery. Forensic Therapist Annual Journal. Vol. 4, pp. 86-104.

Ellis, A. (2001) Overcoming Destructive Beliefs, Feelings, and Behaviors: New Directions for Rational Emotive Behavior Therapy. Prometheus Books.

Ellis, A., and McClaren, C. (2003) Rational Emotive Behavior Therapy: A Therapist's Guide. Impact Publishers.

Ellis, A. (1988) How to stubbornly refuse to make yourself miserable about anything yes, anything! Secaucus, NJ: Lyle Stuart.

Ellis, A. (1977) Anger-How to live with and without it. Carol Publishing Group, New York.

Fisher, G., and Harrison, T. (2000) Substance Abuse: Information for School Counselors, Social Workers, Therapists and Counselors. 2nd ed. Massachusetts: Allyn and Bacon.

Flores, P.J. (1997) Group Psychotherapy with Addicted Populations: An Integration of Twelve-Step and Psychodynamic Theory. 2d ed. New York: The Haworth Press.

Friedman, W.H. (1985) Practical Group Therapy: A Guide for Clinicians. San Francisco: Jossey-Bass.

Glasser, W. (1965) Reality Therapy: A New Approach to Psychiatry. New York: Harper and Row.

Gorski, T.T. (1990) The Cenaps Model of Relapse Prevention: Basic Principles and Procedures. Journal of Psychoactive Drugs, 22, 125-133.

Holmes, P., Georgescu, S., and Liles, W. (2005) Further Delineating the Applicability of Acceptance and Change to Private Responses: The Example of Dialectical Behavior Therapy. The Behavior Analyst Today. 7, 3, pp. 301-311.

Levin, P. (1977) Women's Oppression. Transactional Analysis Journal. Vol. 7, No. 1.

Linehan, M.M., and Dimeff, L. (2001) Dialectical Behavior Therapy in a Nutshell. The California Psychologist, 34, 10-13.

Little, G.L., and Robinson, K.D (1988) Moral Reconation Therapy: a systematic step-by-step treatment system for treatment resistant clients. Psychological Reports, 62, pp. 135-151.

Little, G.L. (2001) Meta-analysis of MRT recidivism research on post-incarceration adult felony offenders, Cognitive-Behavioral Treatment Review, 10, 3, pp. 4-6.

Little, G.L. (2000) Cognitive Behavioral Treatment of Offenders: A Comprehensive Review of MRT Outcome Research. Addictive Behaviors Treatment Review, Vol.2, No.1. pp. 12-21.

Marziali, E., Munroe-Blum H., McLeary L. (1997) The Contributions of group cohesion and group alliance to the outcome of group psychotherapy. International Journal of Group Psychotherapy, 47, 4, pp. 475-497.

Merlo, A., and Pollock, J. (1995) Women, Law, and Social Control. Boston: Allyn and Bacon.

Messina, N., Burdon, W., and Prendergast, M. (2001) A profile of women in prison based therapeutic communities. Draft. Los Angeles: UCLA Integrated Substance Abuse Program. Research Center.

Miller, W.R., and Rollnick, S. (1991) Motivational Interviewing: Preparing People to Change Addictive Behavior. New York: Guilford Press.

Maultsby, M.C (1984) Rational Behavior Therapy. Englewood Cliffs, NJ: Prentice-Hall.

Novaco, R. (1975) Anger Control. Lexington Books, Lexington, MS.

Pollock-Byrne, J.M (1990) Women, prison and crime. Pacific Grove, CA: Brooks/Cole.

Paschal, B.B. (1975) Termination and the Autonomy Chair. Transactional Analysis Journal, Vol. 5. No. 2.

Prochaska, J.O., and DiClemente, C.C. (1983). Stages and Processes of self-change of smoking: Toward an integrative model of change. Journal of Consulting and Clinical Psychology, 51, 390-395.

Prochaska, J.O. (1994). Strong and weak principles for progressing from precontemplation to action on the basis of twelve problem behaviors. Health Psychology, 13, 47-51.

Prochaska, J.O., and Velicer, W.F. (1997). The Transtheoretical Model of health behavior change. American Journal of Health Promotion, 12, 38-48.

Rollnick, S., and Miller, W.R. (1995) What is Motivational Interviewing? Behavioral and Cognitive Psychotherapy. 23:325-334.

Rutan, J.S., and Stone, W.N. (2001) Psychodynamic Group Psychotherapy. 3rd ed. New York: Guilford Press.

Yalom, I.D. (1995) The Theory and Practice of Group Psychotherapy. 4th ed. New York: Basic Books.

Miller, W.R., and Rollnick, S. (1995) Motivational Interviewing: Preparing People to Change Addictive Behavior. New York: Guilford Press.

Miller, M.L,; and Hobler, B. (1996) Delaware's Life Skills Program reduces inmate recidivism. Corrections Today, 58, 5, pp. 114-118.

About the Author

Dr. Francis J. Deisler is a Licensed Clinical Social Worker, Licensed Marriage and Family Therapist, Licensed Psychologist, and a Certified Alcohol and Drug Abuse Counselor in private practice. He is an ex-offender and recovering addict with almost forty years of being criminal justice and drug free. He works extensively with the courts, probation and parole departments, and various prisons in numerous states. He has been recognized for his work with offenders and their families by being awarded the Distinguished Hoosier Award by then Indiana Governor Evan Bayh, The Honorary Secretary of State Award by Indiana Secretary of State Joseph Hogsett, and commissioned as a Kentucky Colonel by Kentucky Governor Paul Patton. He has received numerous letters and proclamations from court systems and law enforcement agencies throughout the United States.